AUTHENTIC TASTES OF
Southeast Asia

CELINE CARNEGIE

NEW
HOLLAND

Published in 2014 by
New Holland Publishers
London • Sydney • Cape Town • Auckland

The Chandlery Unit 114 50 Westminster Bridge Road London SE1 7QY UK
1/66 Gibbes Street Chatswood NSW 2067 Australia
Wembley Square First Floor Solan Road Gardens Cape Town 8001 South Africa
218 Lake Road Northcote Auckland New Zealand

www.newhollandpublishers.com

A catalogue record of this book is available at the British Library and the National Library of Australia.

ISBN: 9781742575483

Managing Director: Fiona Schultz
Publisher: Fiona Schultz
Design: Lorena Susak
Production Director: Olga Dementiev
Printer: Toppan Leefung Printing Ltd (China)

10 9 8 7 6 5 4 3 2 1

Follow New Holland Publishers on
Facebook: www.facebook.com/NewHollandPublishers

Contents

Introduction

On my travels in Southeast Asia I revelled in the fabulous food served at street stalls and tiny family run restaurants and would always wish I could get into the kitchens to see how it was prepared! Back at home, I often tried to recreate the dishes I had enjoyed and cooked many memorable meals as a result. However, while guests graciously complimented the meal, I never really felt that I had captured the same flavours I had experienced. Were the ingredients used in Southeast Asia different from those I could obtain at home? Had the recipes I was using been adapted to suit western tastes? Or was there something in the methods used in those tiny kitchens and stalls that made the difference?

Apart from some slight variations in the ingredients used (for example, the garlic and shallots seem a little milder in Southeast Asia than those at home), the reason I found difficulty in recreating the authentic taste of Asian food at home was as a result of the slightly westernised recipes and the methods I was using.

Using the cookbook and recipes

Southeast Asian food is very easy to cook though I recommend that you read through a recipe before starting to cook to get an overall idea of what will be involved. It is important to be well organised. Many Southeast Asian dishes are very quick to cook so the ingredients should be prepared in advance and ready to use.

If there are suitable substitutes for any ingredients I have listed them at the end of each recipe along with suggested variations. For further information on a particular ingredient please refer to the glossary of essential or unusual ingredients provided. It is a good idea to become familiar with the ingredients you will be using.

Cooking Southeast Asian food is economical. The ingredients tend to stretch further, as often only small amounts of several ingredients are used in a recipe. For instance a delicious Thai salad or a simple stir-fried seafood noodle dish requires only a few shrimp and a few pieces of squid per person and a small piece of leftover Sweet Roast Pork or Char Siew can be used to make fantastic noodle soups.

The methods used by cooks all over Southeast Asia are reflected in the recipes in this cookbook. In many cases our cooks had no electricity or electrical equipment so the methods used were sometimes more time-consuming than if that equipment was available. At the end of some recipes I have listed some shortcuts that can be taken without significantly affecting the quality of the finished dish.

Glossary of essential or unusual ingredients

Andaliman
This spice is a berry unique to northern Sumatra and widely used in spice pastes there. It is also called *intir-intir*. There is no formal English name although it is sometimes referred to as 'jungle pepper'. It has a lemony, peppery flavour that, if eaten on its own, creates a tingling, numbing sensation in the lips. I find crushed lemongrass and black peppercorns an acceptable substitute.

Basil
There are three main varieties of Asian basil used in Thai cooking: holy basil (*bai kaphrao* in Thai), Thai basil (*bai horaphaa*, the type of basil most similar to sweet basil) and lemon basil (*bai maenglak*). Basil is used in many dishes including curries, stir-fries and salads. When used in a cooked dish the basil leaves are usually added at the last minute, as the heat of the already cooked food is enough to wilt them. While Asian food stores will usually have two or more varieties, sweet basil is readily available and is a passable substitute. The easiest way to have a ready supply of Asian basil (for at least part of the year) is to grow it from mixed basil seeds. The different basils can be substituted for each other without making too much difference to the overall flavour.

Bean Paste
See Soybean Paste.

Candle Nuts
Candle nuts are used extensively in Indonesia and Malaysia where they are called *kemiri* and *buah keras* respectively. They are round (about the size of a marble) and quite hard but with a slightly crumbly texture. They are mainly used as a binding and flavouring agent in spice pastes. In my opinion, the closest substitutes are macadamia nuts (in the same quantity) or blanched almonds (using two whole almonds or a teaspoon of ground almonds per candle nut). Candle nuts are available in some supermarkets (usually in the Asian food section) and in Asian food stores.

Chicken Seasoning Powder
This flavouring ingredient is used to enhance flavours. It is available at Asian food stores and some supermarkets; Knorr is a popular brand.

Chillies
There are three main varieties of chillies used in Asian cooking. Tiny bird's eye chillies (3/8–1 1/4 in/1–3 cm) are the hottest type and are used in abundance throughout Southeast Asia. Next are the longer, slender chillies (2 1/4 –3 in/6–8 cm), which, although not quite as hot, can still be very fiery; the red variety are often dried and used in red curry pastes. The third type is the larger and fatter (4 3/4–5 1/2 in/12–14 cm) chillies, which are not as hot as the other two and are also often used in dried form. Recipes may call for either green or red variations of each variety, depending on what flavour is required.

In Asia, chillies are frequently used unseeded. To reduce the hotness of a dish, the seeds and membrane (the hottest part) can be removed or larger chillies can be substituted for smaller ones. This will not make too much difference to the overall flavour of the dish. Chillies freeze well and will thaw in a few seconds when run under a cold tap, although the quality is not quite as good as when they are used fresh. Note: when frying chillies or anything that contains chillies avoid using very high temperatures, as the fumes created by burning chillies are quite unpleasant.

Coconut and Coconut Milk
Just about every part of the versatile coconut is used in Southeast Asia. The juice or water of young coconuts is widely consumed as a drink. The flesh of young coconuts is a deliciously refreshing fruit while the flesh of older fruit is used mainly to make coconut milk, cream and oil. Coconut flesh is also often grated (shredded) (toasted or untoasted) for use in a variety of dishes. The coconut is an

essential ingredient in Southeast Asian cooking – even the fibrous husks are used as charcoal for cooking fires. Coconut cream and milk are made by soaking freshly grated coconut in hot water. The settled top layer of the first straining produces coconut cream and the subsequent soakings and strainings produce coconut milk. Freshly made coconut milk and cream are superior to canned or packaged products, but it is not an easy task and nearly always ends with grated knuckles! There are several brands of coconut milk and cream available in cans and cartons. Canned coconut milk is often quite thick so if a recipe calls for thin coconut milk, it may need to be thinned with water to the consistency of full cream milk. If coconut cream is called for, use the thick layer that rises to the top of the can when given time to settle.

To make fresh coconut milk, first buy a coconut that contains plenty of water and has no mouldy spots. Hold it in your palm over a sink and hit it in the centre with the back of a heavy knife or cleaver. Turn it and hit again and repeat until it cracks. Place the 2 halves in a low oven for 15–20 minutes, which makes it easier to remove the flesh. Carefully use a small knife to cut through portions of flesh and then prise the pieces away from the shell. Grate the flesh finely. Soak the flesh in hot water for 10 minutes in a ratio of 2 cups (16 fl oz/475 ml) hot water per coconut. Squeeze the flesh well with clean hands, then strain through a fine sieve. You can repeat the process up to twice more. Coconut milk must be used within 2 days.

Coriander and Saw Leaf Coriander
Fresh coriander (cilantro) leaves, stems and roots are used extensively in Thai cooking while the seeds are used in most Asian cuisines. There is no substitute for fresh coriander, but ground coriander is the obvious substitute when seeds are called for. Coriander is easy to grow and the seeds can be harvested for further plantings or for using in the kitchen. Saw leaf coriander (also called perennial coriander) is used in some Thai salads. It has a similar flavour to ordinary coriander and has elongated, serrated leaves.

Crispy Fried Garlic
Crispy fried garlic is used throughout Southeast Asia and in particular Thailand as both an ingredient and as a garnish. Packaged crispy fried garlic is available from Asian food stores and is adequate, although homemade crispy fried garlic is better and keeps well in an airtight container. *See* the Crispy Fried Garlic recipe.

Crispy Fried Shallots
Crispy fried shallots are also popular throughout Southeast Asia, and are primarily used as a garnish. To make, fry thinly sliced shallot bulbs in the same way as crispy fried garlic. They will only stay crisp for a couple of days at most. Packaged crispy fried shallots are available from Asian food stores and many supermarkets, and will stay crisp for several weeks when stored in an airtight container.

Dried Shrimp
Dried shrimp is very popular in Thailand. The tiny whole bright orange or pink variety is the most popular. Similar varieties are available in most Asian food stores and, although they are adequate, I find that they are not quite as good as those used in Thailand. Also available are larger shelled and dried shrimp tails, which are orange in colour, quite hard, and tend to have a more pungent flavour. They are not a suitable substitute for whole dried shrimp; they are better suited to being ground into shrimp floss or powder. Some Asian food stores stock tiny, shelled dried shrimp tails, which are a good substitute for whole dried shrimp. They are about ¼ in (5 mm) long, are bright orange or pink and are relatively soft. They need to be kept refrigerated and used within the time indicated on the packet.

Fish Sauce
Fish sauce (*nam pla* in Thai) is almost always found on the tables of restaurants in Thailand, usually with sliced bird's eye chillies floating in it for use as a seasoning condiment. It is now easily available in most supermarkets (usually in the Asian food section) and in all Asian food stores. There is no good substitute. Some people find the strong smell offensive, but don't be put off by it. Fish sauce is indispensable in Thai cooking and, when added to a dish completely changes and enhances the taste without making it taste like fish sauce.

Fish Balls and Fish Cakes

Fish balls are used all over Southeast Asia in soups, stir-fries and curries. They are available either fresh or frozen from most Asian food stores and all Asian fish markets. Generally fish balls are made of minced (ground) fish, but flavour enhancers are sometimes added, so it is advisable to check the ingredients on the packet for any possible allergens. Fish cakes are similar to fish balls in taste but are shaped into small flat patties and are deep-fried. They are not as easily available as fish balls.

Galangal

Galangal is widely used in Thailand and Indonesia where it is called *khaa* and *laos* respectively. It belongs to the ginger family but is milder in flavour than root ginger. It is available dried or powdered and although these can be substituted (as a last resort), fresh galangal is far superior. It is becoming more readily available in fresh or frozen form, but usually only in Asian food stores. If you buy fresh galangal, cut it into pieces and freeze it to have a ready supply. I find that half the quantity of fresh ginger is a good substitute. It will result in a slightly different but still delicious flavour.

Garam Masala

This is an Indian spice blend usually containing coriander (cilantro), cumin, cardamon, cinnamon, pepper, cloves and nutmeg. It is frequently added to dishes toward the end of cooking. It is fairly strong so only a small amount is needed.

Garlic

In my experience, the garlic most widely used in Asia has very small cloves and the flavour seems to be slightly milder than the garlic available in western countries. Since the size of garlic cloves in general vary, I have (where appropriate) given the quantities in teaspoons, tablespoons or cup portions. 1 clove of garlic equals roughly 1 teaspoon.

Garlic Chives

Used in many Thai dishes, these chives have flat leaves and a mild garlic flavour. They grow quite easily in most climates. Ordinary chives or the green tops of spring onions (scallions) can be substituted without making too much difference to the flavour.

Kaffir Lime

The leaves and zest of the kaffir lime are more widely used than the fruit. The leaves have a unique lemony flavour synonymous with Thai cooking and are also used in Indonesian and Malaysian dishes. The leaves are usually available in Asian food stores either dried or frozen and sometimes fresh; frozen or fresh leaves are far superior to the dried ones. The whole fruit do not seem to be very easily available. The best way to have a ready supply is to grow a tree, climate permitting. Finely grated (shredded) lime or lemon zest provide a passable but not ideal substitute for kaffir lime leaves or zest.

Kencur

In Indonesia, *kencur* is used almost as much as ginger and galangal. It is a rhizome and looks a bit like fresh turmeric except that the flesh is white. It has a strong, almost camphor-like flavour very similar to that of *krachai*, a root used in Thailand. Some publications call this root lesser galangal while others refer to it as zedoary or resurrection lily. The Thai name is *prok hom* or *pro hom*. In my experience it is not readily available outside of Asia and I have successfully substituted galangal using half the quantity.

Krachai

This rhizome consists of clumps of long, pencil-like roots and is a familiar sight in the markets of Thailand. It is often called 'Chinese keys' in English. It has a strong camphor-like flavour similar to the Indonesian root called *kencur*. I have seen it being julienned and used in a red curry fish stir-fried dish. It is available frozen in some Asian food stores but the frozen root is not an acceptable substitute in a stir-fry. I have successfully substituted julienned ginger root.

Lemongrass

Lemongrass is becoming a common item in supermarkets and is available in all Asian food stores. It can be grown. Whole stalks are sometimes used to flavour soups or curries. To stop a stalk breaking up and to release more flavour, bruise it well on two sides then tie it in a double knot. Finely sliced or pounded, the bottom white part (usually about 4 in/10 cm) of the stalk is used in many salads and curry pastes.

Lime

Fresh lime juice plays a major part in Thai cuisine. Lemon juice can be substituted though the flavour of the final dish will be a little different. Bottled lime juice, available from supermarkets, is a reasonable substitute.

MSG

Monosodium glutamate (MSG) (known as *aji-ni-moto* in Malaysia, *phong chew rot* in Thailand and 'tasty' [!] in Indonesia) is a flavouring aid that is widely used throughout Asia. I believe that the reason for this is that it is so aggressively marketed there that many people think they need it. In my opinion most of the foods of Asia contain so many delicious flavours that the addition of MSG is completely unnecessary.

Noodles

There are a huge variety of noodles available on the market. The best selections of fresh noodles are usually found in Asian food stores although the round egg noodles (Hokkien or Singapore noodles) are often found in the refrigerated section of supermarkets. Thin egg noodles or wonton noodles are usually available in 2 varieties; round or flat. The fresh varieties usually come packaged in bundles with a light coating of flour, and keep very well in the freezer. A good alternative to fresh thin egg noodles is the dried wheat noodles available in many supermarkets. They are packaged in tight bundles and should be soaked in warm water to loosen them before cooking. Rice noodles come in several shapes and sizes. Fresh rice noodles are available at most Asian food stores although the dried ones are more easily available. Rice vermicelli are very thin, round noodles. Rice sticks are flat and come in a variety of thicknesses: thin ones for dishes such as *Pad Thai* or Thai Fried Noodles and thick ones for *Fried Koay Teow* or Malaysian Fried Noodles. Glass noodles, also called cellophane or bean thread noodles, are the type most commonly used in Thai salads and as part of the filling for spring rolls.

Oil

Throughout Southeast Asia, coconut oil is widely used but generally vegetable, sunflower or canola oils are quite adequate. Peanut oil is also very good. When deep-frying small items, the oil temperature should be 180–190°C (355–375°F). To check that the oil is at the correct temperature, it is a good idea to cook just one item first or throw in a small cube of bread. If it sizzles immediately, the oil is ready for deep-frying.

Pandan Leaves

The long narrow green pandan leaves are used to flavour both sweet and savoury dishes. The aroma is soimilar to vanilla. Pandan leaves are also used to make an essence that is used as both a flavouring and colouring agent. The English name for the leaves is screwpine, and they are usually available frozen in Asian food stores. I have found that in most cases omitting them does not greatly affect the overall result.

Palm Sugar

Palm sugar is widely used in Indonesia where it is sold in blocks and called *gula merah* or *gula jawa*. It is dark brown and quite hard. The palm sugar available in Thailand is called *namtaan pip* and is much lighter in colour and softer in texture, though still quite hard in cool climates. Try to use the appropriate type for a truly authentic taste; however the various types of palm sugar are interchangeable. In cooler climates, when the sugar is very hard, it can be shaved or grated (shredded) or heated in the microwave for a few seconds to soften it. Palm sugar is usually available in all Asian food stores and some supermarkets. Soft brown sugar is an acceptable substitute.

Pea Eggplants

Pea eggplants (aubergines) are a small, round green Thai vegetable used mainly in curries. They have a bitter flavour that mellows when cooked with a curry. They are available in some vegetable shops but, in my experience, not on a regular basis. While pea eggplants contribute to an authentic Thai curry, ordinary eggplant or any other vegetable of choice can be used in curries instead.

Peanuts

Both whole and finely crushed peanuts are used extensively in Thailand, either as a garnish, accompaniment or in cooked dishes such as curries. The peanuts are almost always roasted and left unsalted. Although any unsalted roasted peanuts can be used in Thai cooking, I prefer the small red-skinned peanuts that are available in most Asian food stores. If you cannot find unsalted roasted peanuts then buy some raw peanuts and roast them either in the oven or in a dry wok (*see* the Roasted Peanuts recipe). The flavour of home-roasted peanuts is often far better than commercial ones. Peanuts are also used in other Southeast Asian cuisines and are the main ingredient in satay sauce.

Pickled Garlic

Pickled garlic is used in Thailand to sharpen the flavour of salads and noodle dishes. The sliced cloves and/or the flavoured liquid can be used. Picked garlic is available in Asian food stores.

Salam Leaves

Salam leaves, or *daun salam* in Indonesian, are widely used throughout Indonesia in much the same way as bay leaves are used in western cuisines. They can sometimes be found in Asian food stores. There is some conflicting information regarding suitable substitutes. If unavailable, they can be omitted without making too much difference. I usually substitute bay leaves.

Salted Radish

Salted radish is a preserved vegetable that provides a salty flavour to soups and other dishes. In Thailand, it is widely used in *Pad Thai*, the most popular fried noodle dish. It is available in Asian food stores in vacuum packs and, once opened, should be stored in a jar in the refrigerator. It can keep for several months.

Seasoning Sauce

This is mainly used in Thailand. The Thai brands are milder but saltier in taste than the Maggi or Knorr brands usually available in supermarkets, so it is worthwhile searching for a Thai brand in Asian food stores. Light soy sauce is an acceptable substitute and preferable to the non-Thai brands of seasoning sauce.

Shallots

These are small brown or reddish-skinned onions with a red tinge to the flesh. They usually grow in clusters of 4 or 5 shallots. The flavour is similar to onions but stronger. If necessary, onions can be substituted. Since the size of shallots vary greatly, the quantities for recipes in this book are given in cups, tablespoons or teaspoons as well as numbers of segments. 1 shallot segment equals roughly 2 teaspoons.

Shrimp Paste

Widely used throughout Asia, this pungent and, some would say, foul-smelling paste is essential to obtain an authentic Asian flavour. Like fish sauce, the taste of shrimp paste is far different from its strong smell once it has been mixed or pounded with other ingredients. It is usually used in quite small amounts. The type used in Thailand (*ka-pi*) is a bit lighter in colour and softer in texture than the darker, harder type used in Indonesia (*terasi*) and Malaysia (*blachan*), so for authenticity try to use the one recommended in the recipe if at all possible. *Terasi* or *blachan* is usually toasted before using. Shrimp paste is available in some supermarkets and all Asian food stores. Keep it in a tightly sealed jar or container to avoid stinking out your pantry!

Soybean Paste

This is a paste or thick sauce made from ground soybeans, water, sugar and salt, also called ground bean paste or bean paste. It is dark brown in colour and tastes very salty, so there is no need to add salt to dishes that use it. I recommend Tung Chun brand.

Soy Sauce

The main varieties used in Southeast Asian cooking are the following: light soy sauce (also called white or thin soy sauce), which is very thin and light in colour; dark soy sauce, which is thin and black; sweet soy sauce (*kecap manis* in Indonesian), which is thick, sweet and black; salty soy sauce (*kecap asin* in Indonesian), which is thin and quite dark in colour; thick black soy sauce, also sold as 'caramel sauce', which is thick but not as sweet as *kecap manis*.

Stock

Chicken, pork or a combination of chicken and pork stock is used extensively throughout Southeast Asia. Stocks form the basis of many soups and are also added to other dishes in varying quantities. A simple chicken stock can be made using 2¼ lb (1 kg) of chicken carcasses. Wash them well, remove the 'tail' and place in a large pot. Add a knob of bruised ginger, a few coriander roots, a quartered, unpeeled brown onion, a teaspoon of salt and water to cover. Bring to the boil and skim the surface. Reduce heat and add ½ teaspoon black peppercorns then cover and simmer for 1 hour. Cool and strain. There is a Thai pork stock recipe included here.

Sweet Turnip

Also called yam bean, this is the vegetable used to make the popular Chinese fresh spring rolls called *Popiah*. Yam beans are quite large and shaped a little like a minaret, with creamy white, sweet flesh and brownish or white skin. White radish could be substituted although extra sugar would need to be added.

Tamarind

The tamarind tree is a huge, slow-growing tree found in tropical climates. The fruits are long dark brown pods that contain a pulpy mass of fibres, flesh and seeds. Tamarind is available in blocks that include pulp, fibres and seeds or as a prepared paste, which can be diluted if necessary. To make tamarind liquid, the contents of the pod or pulp is mixed with and soaked in warm or hot water and then strained through a coarse sieve or simply drained, holding back the seeds and fibres. The higher the proportion of pulp to water, the thicker the liquid will be. Tamarind provides a sour flavour and a little lemon juice is an acceptable, though not ideal, substitute. Dried tamarind skin is used to flavour some simmered dishes.

Turmeric

Fresh turmeric root is widely used throughout Southeast Asia. It is usually pounded into spice pastes. It freezes well and is becoming more widely available in Asian food stores and vegetable shops. To freeze turmeric, first cut it into pieces and store in a plastic container. Fresh turmeric has similar keeping qualities to fresh ginger. Most of the time ground turmeric can be substituted at approximately half of the fresh quantity. Note: Fresh turmeric will stain at even the slightest touch so take care unless you want yellow hands and clothes! Stains on benches or utensils can usually be removed using a cream cleanser.

Equipment and Utensils

The majority of Asian dishes can be cooked using very simple equipment. Ovens are rare while gas burners and charcoal fires (barbecues) are widely used. Likewise, electrical equipment, with the exception of rice cookers, is not used a great deal. Most of the grinding of herbs, spices and vegetables for spice pastes and sambals (sauces) is done with mortar and pestle or on grinding stones. Grinding stones are widely used in Indonesia where they are called cobek (pronounced 'cho-bek'). Following is some information on essential or very useful equipment and suggested alternatives.

The Wok

As most people know, the wok is indispensable in Asian cooking. It is ideally shaped for stir-frying and can double as a steamer, deep-fryer or pot. The relatively thin material makes for quick adjustment of heat which is particularly useful for when you need to add several sauces: you just lower the heat so the food does not burn, add whatever you need, then increase the heat and continue with the recipe. Woks undeniably work better over a gas flame as an electric element does not heat enough of the surface of the wok. If you only have electric elements and are serious about Asian cooking, it is worthwhile investing in a gas bottle and burner or a good electric wok.

New steel woks must be seasoned before use or they will rust easily and food will stick. Seasoning creates a non-stick protective coating. To season a wok, first wash it in hot soapy water with a nylon scourer. Rinse and allow it to dry naturally. Now heat the wok until very hot and add 1 teaspoon of oil, preferably peanut oil. Rub the oil over the surface of the wok with a wad of paper towel until absorbed. Repeat using new paper towel until the towel is relatively clean after rubbing. The wok is now ready for use. If you don't use it every day, it is advisable to coat the surface with a little oil before storing to provide extra protection against rust. Never scrub the wok with a scourer again. After cooking, pour in some water then wash in soapy water and rinse as soon as possible. The wok should be completely dry before oiling and storing.

Another point to bear in mind when using your wok is not to overheat it before cooking some foods. A hot wok will splatter when a spice paste is added, and the fumes from burning chillies is particularly unpleasant.

Spatula

A flat, shovel-shaped metal spatula, available inexpensively in Asian food stores, is perfect to use with a wok as it is specially shaped for this purpose. Alternatively, use a wooden spatula, preferably with a rounded end.

Mortar or Grinding Stone (Cobek) and Pestle

To cook truly authentic Asian food it is well worthwhile investing in one or both of these utensils, which are easily available and inexpensive at Asian food stores. Many Asian cooks and chefs firmly believe that a better result is obtained by grinding pastes, spices etc. with a mortar and pestle or on a grinding stone than in an electric food processor. In my opinion, there are two reasons for this: firstly, the stone pestle or *ulek-ulek* or *alu* (the pestle used with a *cobek*) releases the oils in herbs and spices more effectively than the metal blade of a food processor or blender. Secondly, the ingredients are ground to slightly different extents with the pestle, thereby creating a paste with a variety of textures rather than the uniform texture usually obtained using a food processor. That being said, there is a time difference between using a mortar and pestle and grinding paste with a food processor. The difference in quality of the end result is probably not big enough to dismiss the food processor completely. If using one the best result is usually obtained when processing a large quantity so it may be worth doubling or tripling quantities and storing the leftover spice paste. When processing, use the pulse button and scrape down the sides regularly. Another option is to finely chop the tougher ingredients in a food processor and finish the spice paste with a mortar and pestle.

Steamers

There are a few ways of steaming food in Asian cooking. The purpose-made aluminium or stainless steel steamers are excellent, especially for cooking large items such as whole fish or larger quantities of other foods that cannot be piled on top of each other. They are also relatively inexpensive. Much cheaper though, are bamboo steamers that sit on top of a pan or a steaming plate, which sits on top of the wok. As long as the wok has a tight-fitting lid this is great as it makes quite a large steamer. The final option is a western-type double-saucepan steamer, which is not as useful as the space is usually small and more suitable for vegetables.

Barbeques

For grilling (broiling) Asian foods such as satays, whole fish or chicken, wood coals are best and the coals should not be too hot. Cook over black rather than red-hot coals. Gas barbecues and charcoal burners can also be used.

Cleavers and knives

Steel cleavers or choppers are great for chopping all types of ingredients especially whole chickens or other meats. However, a good quality, sharp cook's knife and a small sharp paring knife are adequate substitutes.

Wire Baskets

These utensils, with their long wooden handles, are very useful in Asian cooking. First there are the shallow ones, which come in several sizes. They are great for draining deep-fried foods and skimming stocks (line with a piece of muslin for better skimming). A large perforated spoon will do the same job. Secondly, the deep (tumbler-shaped) baskets are great for cooking fresh or softened dried noodles; just about every Asian noodle cook uses one. Most noodles cook very quickly so it is easy enough to cook one serving at a time in a noodle basket. You simply place the noodles into the basket, lower into hot or boiling water for the required time, lift out, drain, rinse, drain again and put into the serving bowl. Both types of wire basket are inexpensive and available in Asian food stores and some supermarkets.

Thailand

Thailand – Introduction

Good food and the art of cooking are two of the more important parts of life in Thailand. Thai people definitely live to eat rather than eat to live.

Thai food encompasses a wide range of flavours with the main ones being hot, sweet, sour and salty. The hot flavour is provided by chilli, the sweet by any kind of sugar, the sour by lime juice or vinegar and the salty by fish sauce. These flavours are adjusted according to personal taste. This is made easy in Thailand where just about every meal is automatically served with a condiment holder containing the above ingredients.

A typical Thai meal (in Thailand) would consist of a soup (*tom*), a curry (*kaeng*), a spicy salad (*yam*), a vegetable dish (*phak*), perhaps a meat or seafood dish and, of course, rice (*khao*).

Meals are almost always shared and all of the dishes served simultaneously. Exceptions to the shared meal are the one-plate dishes (where a curry or a meat, seafood or vegetable stir-fry is served on a bed of rice) or the noodle dishes, which may consist of egg or rice noodles prepared either in a soup or a dry version of the soup, or stir-fried to make the famous delicious noodle dish *Pad Thai*.

Desserts are not typically served as part of traditional Thai meals. However, sweet snacks, which are made and sold at speciality shops or market stalls, are eaten at any time of the day.

There are four regions within Thailand, each with its own culinary distinctiveness – southern, central, northern and northeastern. The food of the south is influenced by its proximity to Malaysia and tends to be spicier than that of other regions. Central cuisine includes many of the most popular dishes such as red and green curries and *tom yam* soups (*see* recipes). Northern food includes dishes influenced by nearby Burma, such as *kaeng hangleh* (pork curry). The north is also famous for its chilli dips. Northeastern or Issan food includes *Kai Yaang* (marinated grilled (broiled) chicken) which is famous all over Thailand along with *Som Tam* (Green Papaya Salad) and sticky (glutinous) rice.

Common threads linking all the various cuisines throughout Thailand include the extensive use of fresh herbs and roots, hot chillies and pungent *nam pla* (fish sauce), its meticulous presentation and the omnipresence of delicious Thai jasmine rice.

Kai Thawt Bai Toey [Chicken in Pandan Leaves]

This is a popular Thai appetiser that I first had in Chiang Mai many years ago. It is a little bit tricky to make but the chicken does not have to be fully enclosed within a leaf and the result is well worth the effort.

Ingredients

9 oz (250 g) chicken, cut into 3 cm (1¼ in) pieces
About 12 pandan leaves
Small bamboo sticks, or carefully split pieces of bamboo skewer
Vegetable oil, for deep-frying

MARINADE
1 garlic clove, crushed
1 teaspoon oyster sauce
1 teaspoon chilli sauce
2 teaspoons light soy sauce
2 teaspoons fish sauce (nam pla)
1 teaspoon Thai palm sugar
¼ teaspoon white pepper

TO SERVE
Thai sweet chilli sauce

SERVES 2

Method

MARINADE
Mix the marinade ingredients together. Add the chicken and marinate for at least 30 minutes in a non-metallic container.

CHICKEN PARCELS
Place a piece of chicken on the soft end of a pandan leaf and wrap it, samosa-style, folding at right angles over and over until the chicken is enclosed.

Trim the pandan leaf and secure the end with a piece of bamboo stick.

Heat the oil until hot and deep-fry the parcels, a few at a time, for about 5 minutes.

Drain on paper towels and serve with sweet chilli sauce and a bowl for the discarded pandan leaves.

Alternatives & Variations
- Use Indonesian or Malaysian palm sugar instead of Thai.
- Grill (broil) the parcels under medium heat for 15–20 minutes, turning a few times.

Naam Phrik Awng [Chilli Dip with Pork and Tomatoes]

This is one of many popular dips that are specialities of Northern Thailand. It makes an interesting entrée and can also be served as part of a shared meal. In Thailand it is often served with a small basket of sticky (glutinous) rice as well as some raw vegetables for dipping.

Ingredients

CHILLI PASTE
¼ cup large dried chillies, seeds removed, soaked in hot water for 15 minutes
¼ teaspoon salt
4 medium garlic cloves, peeled and roughly chopped
4 shallot segments (about 2 tablespoons), chopped
1 tablespoon vegetable oil

DIP
2 teaspoons vegetable oil
1 garlic clove, minced (crushed)
¼ cup (2 fl oz/60 ml) Chilli Paste (*see* above)
3½ oz (100 g) pork mince
1 large tomato, roughly chopped
½ cup (4 fl oz/125 ml) water
½ tablespoon fish sauce (nam pla)
1 tablespoon coriander (cilantro), chopped
1 tablespoon spring onion (scallion), chopped

GARNISH
1 teaspoon coriander (cilantro) leaves and stems, chopped
1 teaspoon spring onion (scallion), chopped

TO SERVE
Raw white cabbage leaves
Raw green beans, topped and tailed
1 small cucumber, sliced

SERVES 2 AS AN ENTRÉE OR MORE AS PART OF A SHARED MEAL

Method

CHILLI PASTE
Drain the chillies and pound in a mortar and pestle with the salt. Add the garlic and shallots and continue to pound to a fairly smooth paste. Alternatively use a small food processor or blender to make the chilli paste.

Heat a wok over low heat, add the oil and fry the chilli paste for about 4 minutes, or until darker in colour. Remove and store until ready to make the dip or continue with the recipe.

DIP
Heat the vegetable oil in the wok, add the garlic and Chilli Paste and fry for 30 seconds or until aromatic.

Add the mince and stir-fry over high heat, breaking up the meat, for about 30 seconds. Stir in the tomato then add the water and stir again.

Cook over medium-high heat until the tomato is soft and the water evaporated. Add the fish sauce and mix well.

Add the coriander and spring onion, turn off the heat, mix through and spoon into a serving bowl. Garnish with the extra coriander and spring onion. Serve with the raw vegetables.

> Alternatives & Variations
> • This dip can also be served with sticky (glutinous) rice.

Paw-Pia Thawt [Thai Vegetable Spring Rolls]

Vegetable spring rolls are universally available now. Making your own and eating them fresh is an absolute joy. The quantities can be doubled to make more rolls.

Ingredients

FILLING
1 x 50 g (1¾ oz) packet cellophane or glass noodles
1 teaspoon peanut or vegetable oil
1 teaspoon garlic, minced (crushed)
1 cup (4 oz/125 g) white cabbage, shredded or very finely sliced
1 large handful fresh beansprouts
2 tablespoons carrot, julienned
1 tablespoon oyster sauce
1 teaspoon sugar
1 teaspoon light soy sauce
¼ teaspoon Thai seasoning sauce
1 tablespoon coriander (cilantro) leaves
1 tablespoon chives, chopped
¼ teaspoon dark soy sauce

ROLLS
6 large spring-roll wrappers
Beaten egg or water, to seal
Vegetable oil, for deep-frying

TO SERVE
Thai sweet chilli sauce

MAKES 6 LARGE OR 15 SMALL ROLLS

Method

FILLING
Soak the noodles in hot water for a few minutes, drain well and roughly cut into shorter lengths with scissors.

Heat the wok over medium-low heat and add the oil. Add the garlic and fry for 5 seconds. Add the cabbage, beansprouts and carrot and stir-fry until well combined.

Add the oyster sauce, sugar, light soy sauce and seasoning sauce. Stir for about 20 seconds then add the coriander and garlic chives, noodles and dark soy sauce. Stir-fry for another 30 seconds until well combined then remove to a plate and allow to cool.

ROLLS
Place a spring roll wrapper on a bench or board. Place 2 heaped tablespoons of filling on the lower part, leaving 1¼ in (3 cm) of free space around the edges. (If using square wrappers, use them diagonally).

Fold the lower edge up and over the filling and pull back slightly to compact the filling. Roll over 2 or 3 times (depending upon the size of the wrappers). Fold each side in and continue to roll.

Dampen the top edge with a little beaten egg or water and seal. Place sealed side down on a plate while making the rest of the rolls.

Heat the oil until hot. Fry the rolls for 3–4 minutes, turning a few times, until golden brown. Drain and serve whole or sliced with sweet chilli sauce.

Alternatives & Variations
• Use ordinary chives or the tops of spring onions (scallions) instead of garlic chives.
• Use extra light soy sauce instead of Thai seasoning sauce.

Thawt Man Plaa Thai [Thai Fish Cakes]

This popular Thai recipe makes an ideal appetiser.

Ingredients

500 g (1 lb 2 oz) white, soft-textured fish
 fillets
¼ cup Red Curry Paste (*see* recipe)
1 tablespoon or less water
1½ tablespoons fish sauce (nam pla)
1 tablespoon sugar
1 egg
½ cup (3 oz/85 g) snake or green
 (French) beans, thinly sliced
2 teaspoons kaffir lime leaves, finely
 shredded
Vegetable oil for frying

CHILLI AND CUCUMBER SAUCE
¼ cup (2 fl oz/60 ml) Thai sweet chilli
 sauce
¾–1¼ in/2–3 cm piece cucumber, peeled,
 quartered and thinly sliced

SERVES 4–6 AS AN APPETISER

Method

Skin the fish fillets, then finely chop the flesh. Transfer to a mortar and pestle and pound until fairly smooth.

Add 2 teaspoons of the Red Curry Paste and pound until well combined and the mixture is evenly coloured. Add the remaining curry paste, gradually adding some or all of the water and pound until smooth.

Add the fish sauce and sugar and pound until you have a rubbery-textured stiff paste that forms into a ball. Transfer to a large bowl. Add the egg and mix well. Add the beans and shredded kaffir lime leaves, mixing after each addition.

Using your hand, lift the ball of fish paste and throw it into the bowl several times. This is to ensure that the ingredients are fully incorporated into the fish paste. Cover and refrigerate for at least 1 hour or overnight.

Heat the oil in a wok or deep-fryer until hot. Mix the fish paste again a few times. With oiled fingers, form the paste into small, flat patties and fry for 3–4 minutes, turning once or twice, until golden brown. Drain well. Serve with the Chilli and Cucumber Sauce on the side.

CHILLI AND CUCUMBER SAUCE
Mix together the sweet chilli sauce and thinly sliced cucumber.

Alternatives & Variations
- Use 1 teaspoon of grated (shredded) lime zest instead of kaffir lime leaves or omit altogether.
- Shallow-fry the fish cakes instead of deep-frying, using a pan instead of a wok or deep-fryer.
- Use a commercial red curry paste.
- Make the fish paste in a food processor up to and including the egg stage.

Kuaytiaw Naam Tom Yum

[Rice Noodle Soup with Barbecue Pork, Pork Mince, Peanuts and Green Beans]

The list of ingredients may seem long but the dish is very easy to put together and almost all of the ingredients can be prepared well ahead of time if necessary. The amount of chilli used here produces quite a spicy soup but can be adjusted according to taste or even served separately. There is a dry version of this dish called Kuaytiaw Haeng Sukhothai (*see* recipe).

Ingredients

1 teaspoon fish sauce (nam pla)

2 tablespoons pork mince, formed into 2 small patties

3½ oz (100 g) thin flat rice noodles

½ cup (3 oz/85 g) green beans, sliced diagonally

12 slices Char Siew (barbecue pork, *see* recipe)

3 cups (1¼ pints/750 ml) hot Pork Stock (*see* recipe)

SEASONING INGREDIENTS

2 teaspoons Crispy Fried Garlic (available from Asian food stores or *see* recipe)

1 teaspoon fish sauce (nam pla)

2 teaspoons Thai palm sugar, softened for a few seconds in the microwave, if necessary

2 teaspoons sliced large green chillies in white vinegar (use a small amount of chilli and top up the spoon with vinegar (Naam Som Phrik)

1 tablespoon salted radish, chopped

2 tablespoons unsalted roasted peanuts, finely crushed

2 teaspoons coriander (cilantro) leaves and stems, finely chopped

2 teaspoons spring onions (scallions), finely chopped

¼–1 teaspoon dried chilli flakes

SERVES 2

Method

Mix all the seasoning ingredients together until thoroughly combined.

Bring one large filled pan and a half-filled small pan of water to the boil. Add the first teaspoon of fish sauce and the pork mince to the small pan and simmer for about 2–3 minutes, until cooked through. Drain and discard the cooking liquid.

Add the noodles and beans to the large pot of boiling water. Reduce the heat to medium and cook for about 3 minutes, or until the noodles are soft.

Drain and divide between 2 large, deep soup bowls. Now divide the seasoning ingredients between the bowls, then the barbecue pork and finish by pouring 1½ cups (12 fl oz/350 ml) of hot soup stock over each bowl. Mix gently with chopsticks to combine the flavours and serve immediately.

Alternatives & Variations

- Omit the salted radish, if you like. Add saltiness with extra fish sauce, if necessary.
- Use prepared barbecue pork (char siew), available from Chinese barbecue restaurants.

Naam Sup Muu [Pork Stock]

This stock is used in the recipe for Barbecue Pork and Wonton Noodle Soup (see recipe), however it can be used in other recipes that call for pork stock. It is quite peppery so for other recipes you may like to reduce the quantity of that ingredient.

Ingredients

1 kg (2¼ lb) pork bones
½ tablespoon Crispy Fried Garlic (*see* recipe)
3 large or 4 small coriander (cilantro) roots including 2 in (5 cm) of stems
1½ teaspoons salt, to taste
½ teaspoon white pepper

MAKES ABOUT 9 CUPS (3 PINTS/ 2.1 LITRES)

Method

Place the pork bones in a large pan, cover with water and bring to the boil. Boil for 3 minutes then drain and discard the water.

Fill the pan with cold water to rinse the bones once then drain the pot again. Refill with the 8–10 cups (4–4¼ pints/1.9–2.4 litres) of water to cover the bones again.

Add the remaining ingredients and bring to the boil. Reduce the heat to low and simmer, partly covered, for 1½ hours.

Strain and either use immediately or allow to cool, remove any fat from the surface and refrigerate for up to 5 days, or freeze for up to 3 months.

Alternatives & Variations
• Use pre-packaged Crispy Fried Garlic, available from Asian food stores.

Naam Ba-Mii Kiaw Muu Daeng

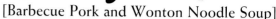

[Barbecue Pork and Wonton Noodle Soup]

The recipe incorporates many elements that can be prepared and made ahead including barbecue pork, the pork gravy, salted radish, fried garlic and soup stock are also used in other recipes. Even the seasonings can be measured into small dishes ready to be added at serving time. Only the noodles and greens must be cooked just before serving.

Ingredients

8 cups (3½ pints/2 litres) Pork Stock
   (*see* recipe)

12 Wontons (*see* recipe)

3 cups (15 oz/420 g) loosely packed thin, fresh egg noodles (also called wonton noodles)

1 cup (4 oz/115 g) Asian greens, sliced into 2 in (5 cm) lengths

40 thin slices Char Siew (barbecue pork, *see* recipe)

1 tablespoon spring onions (scallions), finely chopped

1 teaspoon sugar

2 teaspoons salted radish, chopped (available from Asian food stores)

4 teaspoons Pork Gravy (from the Char Siew recipe)

2 teaspoons Crispy Fried Garlic (*see* recipe)

½ teaspoon white pepper

Serves 4

Method

In a large pan, heat the pork stock until simmering.

Bring another large pan of water to the boil. Add the wontons to the boiling water, reduce the heat to low and simmer very gently for 3–4 minutes, or until the wontons float to the top. Drain and set aside. If you are not using them within a few minutes, toss them in a little oil to prevent them sticking together.

Bring the water to the boil again. Then add the noodles and cook for 30 seconds or according to the packet instructions. If you have a noodle-cooking basket you will probably find it easier to cook one serve at a time. Drain, dunk into cold water or run under the cold tap, drain again and place in the serving bowls.

Add the greens to the hot stock and cook for 2 minutes. Meanwhile, divide the wontons, slices of pork, spring onions, sugar, salted radish, pork gravy, fried garlic and white pepper between the serving bowls, adding the greens at the last minute.

Fill each bowl with soup, stir gently, and serve immediately with chopsticks and a soup spoon.

Alternatives & Variations
• Salted radish can be omitted, if you like.
• Use thick black soy sauce or sweet soy sauce instead of pork gravy.
• Use dried thin wheat noodles instead of fresh egg noodles.
• Use packaged fried garlic. Available from Asian food stores.
• Use prepared, fresh or frozen wontons and cook according to instructions on the pack.
• Use a commercial pork or chicken stock.

Kung Pad Makam Piek [Shrimp with Sweet Tamarind Sauce]

The combined sweetness of raw and palm sugars and the sourness of tamarind result in an interesting and delicious flavour. The sauce and garnishes can be made well in advance.

Ingredients

Vegetable oil, for deep-frying
10 large whole jumbo shrimp (king prawns), washed and deveined, but shells left on
½ tablespoon vegetable oil, extra
¾ cup (3¾ oz/100 g) onion, thinly sliced lengthways

Tamarind Sauce
1½ tablespoons tamarind pulp
½ cup (4 fl oz/125 ml) hot water
1 tablespoon palm sugar
1 tablespoon raw (demerara) sugar
¼ teaspoon salt
1 teaspoon fish sauce (nam pla)

Garnishes
2 shallot segments, thinly sliced (to make Crispy Fried Shallots)
6 medium thin dried red chillies (to make Crispy Fried Chillies)
Fresh coriander (cilantro) leaves

Serves 2 or as one dish in a shared meal

Method

Crispy Fried Shallots and Crispy Fried Chillies
Heat the deep-frying oil in a wok over medium heat. When hot, deep-fry the shallots for about 2 minutes until crisp and dark golden. Drain and set aside.

Deep-fry the dried chillies for a few seconds until crisp. Drain and set aside to cool.

Tamarind Sauce
Soak the tamarind pulp in the hot water. When cool, mix well, then drain through a coarse sieve.

Place in a small saucepan with all of the remaining sauce ingredients and bring to the boil over medium heat. Stir until the sugar is dissolved. Boil for 1 minute then set aside.

Using the same oil that the garnishes were cooked in, deep-fry the shrimp for about 1 minute until just cooked. Drain and set aside.

In another wok or pan, heat the extra ½ tablespoon of oil. Add the onion and fry for a few seconds over high heat.

Add the prepared sauce, stir and bring to the boil. Add the shrimp and stir-fry for 30 seconds.

Place on a serving dish and garnish with the Crispy Fried Shallots, the Crispy Fried Chillies and the coriander leaves.

Khao Soi [Chiang Mai Chicken Curry Noodles]

Khao Soi is a speciality of Chiang Mai in Northern Thailand. There are 4 stages to the recipe – the marinade, the curry paste, the crispy noodles and the soup. Three of these stages can be made ahead of time and reheated to serve; only the soft noodles must be cooked and added just before serving.

Ingredients

8 chicken drumsticks
1 cup (8 fl oz/250 ml) vegetable oil for deep-frying noodles
9 oz (250 g) fresh flat egg noodles (also called wonton noodles)
2 tablespoons Red Curry Paste (see below)

MARINADE
2 teaspoons sugar
2 teaspoons whisky
1 teaspoon Thai seasoning sauce
½ teaspoon mild curry powder

RED CURRY PASTE
6 large red dried chillies, seeded and chopped
6 medium thin red dried chillies, chopped
10 garlic cloves
2 stalks lemongrass (white part only), roughly sliced
10 shallot segments, roughly chopped
2 tablespoons galangal, roughly chopped
1 teaspoon Thai shrimp paste
½ teaspoon mild curry powder

SOUP
1¾ cups (14 oz/ 400 g) coconut cream
4 cups (1¾ pints/1 litre) chicken stock
1 tablespoon each celery leaves, coriander (cilantro) leaves and spring onions (scallions), finely chopped
1 teaspoon sugar

TO SERVE
1 lime, quartered
A few peeled, raw shallot segments
1 cup (4 oz/115 g) Pickled Cabbage

Method

MARINADE
Mix all of the marinade ingredients together in a large bowl. Add the drumsticks, coat well with the marinade and leave for 1–2 hours.

RED CURRY PASTE
Place both types of dried chillies in a food processor and process until finely chopped. Add the garlic, lemongrass, shallots and galangal and continue to process until everything is finely chopped.

Transfer to a mortar and pound for 20–30 minutes until you have a thick, slightly wet, evenly coloured paste.

Add the shrimp paste and curry powder and pound until well combined. Set 2 tablespoons of curry paste aside. The remainder can be stored in a screw-top jar in the refrigerator for up to 1 month or frozen for use in other dishes.

CRISPY NOODLES
Heat the oil in a wok until very hot.

Loosen a bundle of noodles. Take a small handful and carefully lower into the oil. Fry for a few seconds then turn over with tongs and fry for a few more seconds until the noodles are light brown and crisp. Drain and set aside. Repeat until you have four bundles.

SOUP
Pour ½ cup (4 fl oz/125 ml) of the coconut cream into a large pan. Turn the heat to medium and bring to the boil.

Add the remaining Red Curry Paste and stir until well combined. Add another ½ cup (4 fl oz/125 ml) of coconut cream and fry, stirring almost constantly for about 3 minutes until fragrant.

Add the marinated drumsticks (discarding the marinade) and the rest of the coconut cream, mix well and bring to the boil, stirring a couple of times. Add the hot stock and salt and stir again.

Reduce heat to low and simmer uncovered for 1–1½ hours, stirring occasionally.

To Serve

Bring a large pan of water to the boil and then reduce the heat to medium. Loosen the remaining noodles and add to the pan. Cook for 30 seconds or according to cooking instructions on the packet. If using a noodle-cooking basket, cook one serve of noodles at a time. Drain and place into four individual large bowls.

Divide the chopped celery, coriander, spring onions and sugar between the bowls. Place 2 drumsticks in each bowl and divide the soup between the bowls. Top each bowl with a bundle of crispy noodles.

On a separate plate, place the wedges of lime, raw shallots and some Pickled Cabbage. Each person adds a squeeze of lime juice, shallots and Pickled Cabbage to their bowl according to taste.

Alternatives & Variations
- Use 2 teaspoons light soy sauce instead of seasoning sauce.
- If fresh galangal is not available, use half the quantity of fresh ginger root. The flavour will be slightly different but still delicious.
- Use Indonesian or Malaysian shrimp paste instead of Thai.
- Make the entire curry paste in a food processor instead of transferring to a mortar. You may need to add a tablespoon of water to assist blending.
- Use prepared red curry paste mixed with ¼ teaspoon of curry powder.

Tom Yam Kung  [Chilli and Lemongrass Soup with Shrimp]

Tom Yam is possibly the most famous of all Thai soups with its hot and sour flavours. To cater for different tastes add the chillies whole and advise guests to crush the chillies within the soup if they want a hotter flavour. Naam Phrik Pao is a paste of fried dried chilli, garlic, shallots, shrimp paste, sugar and fish sauce, which adds a rich red colour and slight oiliness to the soup.

Ingredients

5 cups (2 pints/1.2 litres) water
2 large tomatoes, each cut into 6 wedges
3 stalks lemongrass, sliced diagonally into 1¾ in (4 cm) pieces
1½ tablespoons fish sauce (nam pla), plus 4 teaspoons extra
6–8 kaffir lime leaves, torn into quarters
1½ cups (12 oz/350 g) straw mushrooms (available canned in supermarkets and Asian food stores)
12 large raw shrimp (prawns), shelled and deveined but tails left on
½ tablespoon (or quantity to taste) of mixed red and green bird's eye chillies, crushed or left whole
6 teaspoons lime juice
1 teaspoon sugar
1 tablespoon mint leaves
1 tablespoon coriander (cilantro) leaves
2–4 teaspoons Naam Phrik Pao (*see* recipe)

To Serve
Steamed jasmine rice

Serves 4

Method

Heat the water in a wok or large pan until nearly boiling. Add the tomatoes, lemongrass, fish sauce, kaffir lime leaves and mushrooms. Bring to the boil and allow to boil for 2 minutes. Stir and add the shrimp. Reduce heat to medium.

Gently push the shrimp under the surface of the broth but do not stir at this stage. After about 1 minute, or once the shrimp are cooked, stir gently.

Divide the chillies, soup, shrimp and vegetables between 4 large soup bowls. Season each bowl with quarter of the lime juice, sugar, mint, coriander, extra fish sauce and Naam Phrik Pao.

Stir each bowl gently and serve with steamed jasmine rice.

> **Alternatives & Variations**
> • Use button (whie) mushrooms instead of straw mushrooms.
> • Use 9 oz (250 g) of thinly sliced chicken breast or mixed seafood instead of shrimp.

That Phet Plaa Duk [Fried Fish with Basil and Red Curry Paste]

This is a popular Thai dish that can also be made using chicken, pork or vegetables. This recipe is typically made with catfish cutlets (the Duk in the name!) but any small fish cutlets or firm fillets can be used.

Ingredients

1 lb 11 oz (750 g) small fish cutlets or firm-textured fillets
1 cup (8 fl oz/250 ml) vegetable oil
½ teaspoon garlic, minced (crushed)
1 tablespoon Red Curry Paste (*see* recipe)
1 teaspoon sugar
2 teaspoons fish sauce (nam pla)
½ teaspoon light soy sauce
½ cup krachai, shredded (*see* below)
1 tablespoon green peppercorns, fresh or canned
6–8 kaffir lime leaves, quartered
¼ cup large red chillies, sliced diagonally into large pieces
2 tablespoons water
¾ cup loosely packed holy basil

To Serve
Steamed jasmine rice

Serves 4

Method

If using fish fillets, cut into medium strips or cubes.

Heat the wok over medium-high heat and add the oil. When hot, add the garlic and then the fish. Cook for about 3 minutes (less for fillets) until browned and slightly crisp, turning 2 or 3 times. Remove the fish, drain and set aside.

Carefully pour all but about 2 tablespoons of oil out of the wok into a heatproof container. Heat the wok again over medium heat and add the Red Curry Paste. Fry for a few seconds then add the sugar, fish sauce and light soy sauce. Stir-fry for a few more seconds.

Return the fish to the wok, reduce the heat to medium-low and carefully stir until the fish is coated with curry paste. Add the water and stir carefully to incorporate it then add the krachai, green peppercorns, kaffir lime leaves and chillies. Stir them through and cook for 1 minute.

Add the basil to the wok at the last minute. Mix through, remove from heat and serve with steamed jasmine rice.

Alternatives & Variations
- Krachai is a rhizome (sometimes called lesser galangal) that has a similar but stronger flavour than galangal. It can either be omitted without making too much difference to the taste or replaced with ¼ cup finely julienned ginger for a different but equally delicious flavour.
- Substitute any type of basil for holy basil. The flavour will be slightly different but still delicious.
- Use ½ teaspoon ground black pepper instead of green peppercorns.
- Use a commercial red curry paste.
- Use sliced chicken, pork or a selection of vegetables instead of fish. Stir-fry in 2 tablespoons of oil and remove before adding the curry paste.

Phat Muk Kratiam Phrik Thai

[Fried Squid with Garlic and Pepper]

In Thailand, this dish is more commonly served as a one-plate meal over rice; however it can also be served as part of a shared Thai meal. This recipe is from Koh Kham, a beautiful little island where squid are caught all year round – the squid dishes taste delicious.

Ingredients

3 medium or 6 small squid
1 teaspoon sugar
1 teaspoon Thai seasoning sauce
½ teaspoon fish sauce (nam pla)
3 teaspoons oyster sauce
2 tablespoons vegetable oil
¼ teaspoon ground white pepper
1½ tablespoons Crispy Fried Garlic (*see* recipe)

TO SERVE
Steamed jasmine rice

SERVES 2 OR AS ONE DISH IN A
   SHARED MEAL

Method

PREPARING THE SQUID
If using whole, uncleaned squid, clean them by slitting the tube open and slicing through the head to flatten the whole squid. Scrape out the innards. Remove the head and tentacles and remove the small round 'beak' that is in the centre of the tentacles. Remove the quill from the tube. Wash thoroughly in three changes of water and dry on paper towels.

Cut each squid tube in half and score on the inside, horizontally and vertically. Slice diagonally into strips about ³/₈ in (1 cm) wide. Cut the tentacles into ¾–1¼ in (2–3 cm) lengths and the head section into quarters.

COOKING THE SQUID
Combine the sugar and sauces in a small bowl.

Heat the wok over high heat and add the oil. Add the squid and stir-fry for 20 seconds. Add the sugar and sauce, and stir-fry for 30 seconds. Add the crispy fried garlic and pepper and stir-fry for a further 2 minutes.

Serve immediately over steamed jasmine rice.

Alternatives & Variations
• This dish can also be made with finely chopped pork or chicken. After adding the garlic and pepper, stir-fry until the meat is cooked.
• Buy fried garlic, which is available in packets in Asian food stores.

Neung Plaa Phrik Ma Nao [Steamed Fish with Chilli and Lime]

Variations of this dish can be found all over Thailand. It is one of those recipes that produce a great result for little effort!

Ingredients

1 whole fish (snapper, bream or similar), weighing about 1 lb 2 oz (500 g), cleaned
1 small lime, thinly sliced

Sauce
2 garlic cloves, peeled and roughly sliced
4 bird's eye chillies, red or green, thinly sliced
2 tablespoons lime juice
2 tablespoons fish sauce (nam pla)
1 teaspoon sugar

Garnish
1 tablespoon coriander (cilantro) leaves
1 spring onion (scallion), very thinly sliced lengthways then into 2¼ in (6 cm) pieces

To Serve
Steamed jasmine rice

Serves 4 as part of a shared meal

Method

Place the fish in a steamer basket and arrange the lime slices all over the surface. Steam over high heat for about 15 minutes, or until the thick flesh behind the head is no longer opaque.

Meanwhile, make the sauce and prepare the garnishes.

Sauce
Mix together the garlic, chillies, lime juice, fish sauce and sugar until the sugar is dissolved.

Remove the fish from the steamer and immediately pour the sauce over. Scatter the coriander leaves and spring onion over and serve with steamed jasmine rice.

Alternatives & Variations
• Use lemon juice instead of lime juice.
• For a milder sauce, use 1 large red or green chilli and remove the seeds and membrane.
• Use fish fillets instead of whole fish. Adjust the cooking time according to thickness.

Kaeng Phet Luk Chin Plaa [Red Curry with Fish Balls]

Kaeng phet actually translates as 'hot curry', however the English name is 'red curry' due to the colour of the paste. This one really is hot but for less fire you could reduce the amount of curry paste.

Ingredients

1½ cups (12 fl oz/350 ml) coconut cream
1 cup (8 fl oz/250 ml) Red Curry Paste (*see* recipe)
1 lb 2 oz (500 g) small fish balls
3 cups (1¼ pint/750 ml) thin coconut milk
1½ tablespoons fish sauce (nam pla)
1 tablespoon sugar
½ cup (1¼ oz/35 g) pea eggplants (aubergine)
½ cup large fresh red chillies, seeded and sliced lengthways
½ cup large fresh green chillies, seeded and sliced lengthways
6 fresh kaffir lime leaves, torn into halves or quarters
¾ cup sweet basil leaves

TO SERVE
Steamed jasmine rice

SERVES 4

Method

Pour the coconut cream into a wok or pan. Turn on the heat and bring to the boil. Boil for about 5 minutes, stirring regularly, to prevent burning and boiling over, until the oil starts to separate and rise to the surface.

Add the curry paste, stir well and cook over medium-high heat for 1 minute. Add the fish balls and stir. Cook for 2 minutes, then add the thin coconut milk and cook for 1 minute.

Add the fish sauce, sugar and pea eggplants, and cook for 1 more minute. Add the chillies and kaffir lime leaves and cook for 1 more minute.

Add the basil leaves and remove the pan or wok from the heat. Stir the basil through and serve with steamed jasmine rice.

Alternatives & Variations
- If pea eggplants are not available, use standard eggplant, cubed, or any other vegetables.
- If fresh kaffir lime leaves are not available, use dried leaves (remove before serving), or ordinary lime or lemon leaves.
- This curry can also be made using chicken, beef, pork, any seafood or selection of vegetables. For meat, slice thinly and cook for 5–6 minutes before adding thin coconut milk.
- Use a commercial red curry paste.

Kaeng Khiaw Waan Kai [Green Chicken Curry]

The secret to a delicious Thai curry is to boil the coconut cream until the oil separates then add the curry paste and fry it until fragrant. The addition of extra coconut cream at the end ensures a creamy, smooth-flavoured curry. This curry is fairly hot – to make a milder curry, just use less curry paste.

Ingredients

2¾ cup (1 pint 4 fl oz/675 ml) coconut cream

½ cup (4 fl oz/125 ml) Green Curry Paste (*see* recipe)

1 lb 2 oz (500 g) chicken breast or thigh fillets, thinly sliced

2 tablespoons fish sauce (nam pla)

1 tablespoon sugar

3 cups (1¼ pints/750 ml) thin coconut milk

½ cup (1¼ oz/35 g) pea eggplants (aubergine)

3 large fresh red chillies, seeded and sliced lengthways

3 large fresh green chillies, seeded and sliced lengthways

6 fresh kaffir lime leaves, torn into halves or quarters

1 cup sweet basil leaves

To Serve
Steamed jasmine rice

Serves 4

Method

Pour 2 cups (16 fl oz/475 ml) coconut cream into a wok or pan. Turn on the heat and bring to the boil. Boil for about 5 minutes, stirring regularly, to prevent burning and boiling over, until the oil starts to separate and rise to the surface.

Add the curry paste, stir well and cook for 1 minute over medium-high heat. Add the chicken, fish sauce and sugar, stirring after each addition. Cook for 5–6 minutes, stirring regularly until the oil rises to the surface again.

Add the thin coconut milk, stir and bring to the boil again. Cook for 5 minutes.

Add the eggplant, chillies and kaffir lime leaves and cook for 3 minutes. Add the remaining coconut cream and stir well.

Add the basil leaves, remove from the heat, stir the basil through and serve with steamed jasmine rice.

Alternatives & Variations
- If pea eggplants are not available, use standard eggplant (cubed), or your choice of vegetables. Green beans are particularly good in this curry.
- If fresh kaffir lime leaves are not available, use dried leaves (remove before serving) or ordinary lime or lemon leaves.
- Use a commercial green curry paste.
- This curry can also be made using beef, pork, any seafood or selection of vegetables.

Kaeng Matsaman Kai [Massaman Chicken Curry]

Massaman curry is a sweet yellowish curry, popular in southern Thailand, which takes its name from the Muslims (or Massaman) who brought it to Thailand. It is often made with beef but this chicken version is equally delicious.

Ingredients

1 tablespoon tamarind liquid
   (from 2 teaspoons tamarind pulp, *see* method)
3 cups (1¼ pints/750 ml) coconut cream
3 tablespoons Massaman Curry Paste
   (*see* recipe)
12 oz (350 g) chicken thigh or breast
   fillets, cut into 1¼ in (3 cm) pieces
5 cardamom pods, toasted in a dry pan
   until fragrant
1¾ in (4 cm) cinnamon quill (stick),
   toasted in a dry pan until fragrant
½ teaspoon salt
3 shallot segments (about 1½
   tablespoons), sliced
2 medium potatoes, cut into 1¼ in
   (3 cm) cubes
2 teaspoons fish sauce (nam pla)
3 teaspoons Thai palm sugar
2 tablespoons unsalted roasted peanuts

To Serve
Steamed jasmine rice

Serves 2–3

Method

Make tamarind liquid by soaking 2 teaspoons tamarind pulp in 1½ tablespoons hot water. Stir and strain it when cool and set aside.

Put ½ cup (4 fl oz/125 ml) of the coconut cream into a cold pan or wok and cook over medium heat for 2–3 minutes, or until the oil separates and rises to the surface.

Add the curry paste. Turn the heat to medium-low and when the paste starts to fry, cook for about 2 minutes, or until aromatic. Stir frequently to prevent it burning. Add the chicken and stir to coat with paste.

Add the toasted cardamom pods and cinnamon and fry until the chicken starts to change colour.

Add the remaining coconut cream, salt, shallots and potatoes. Bring to the boil then reduce heat to low and simmer, uncovered, for 30 minutes, stirring occasionally.

Add the fish sauce, 1 tablespoon of the tamarind, palm sugar and peanuts and continue to simmer for 10 more minutes or until the potatoes are cooked.

Serve with steamed jasmine rice.

Alternatives & Variations
• Use onion instead of shallots.
• Use brown sugar instead of palm sugar.
• Use beef or pork instead of chicken.

Kaeng Phet Pet Yaang [Roast Duck Red Curry]

This mild curry from central Thailand is one of many royal dishes that were exclusive to the Thai palace until the late 1960s.

Ingredients

1 cup (8 fl oz/250 ml) coconut cream
2 tablespoons Red Curry Paste (*see* recipe)
½ Chinese-style roast duck, cut or torn into bite-sized pieces
1 cup (8 fl oz/250 ml) coconut milk
½ cup (4 fl oz/120 ml) water
½ cup (3 oz/85 g) pineapple pieces, fresh or canned
2 large seeded red chillies, thinly sliced lengthways
2 tablespoons fish sauce
4 kaffir lime leaves, thinly sliced
2 teaspoons Thai palm sugar

Serves 4

Method

Pour half the coconut cream into a wok or pan. Bring to the boil over medium heat, boil for a few minutes, or until the oil starts to separate then add the curry paste.

Stir and cook for 1–2 minutes until aromatic and oily. Add the duck, coconut milk and water and bring to the boil.

Add the pineapple, chillies, fish sauce, kaffir lime leaves and palm sugar, reduce the heat to low and simmer for a few minutes, or until the duck is heated through.

Stir in the remaining coconut cream and serve with steamed jasmine rice.

Alternatives & Variations
• Use 1 teaspoon shredded lime or lemon peel instead of kaffir lime leaves.

Kai Yaang [Issan Grilled Chicken]

Issan food comes from north-eastern Thailand is often served with Green Papaya Salad (see recipe).

Ingredients

Bamboo skewers (soaked for 30 minutes)
2 lb 4 oz (1 kg) chicken legs and thighs

MARINADE
5 garlic cloves
½ teaspoon salt
2 teaspoons black peppercorns
½ cup coriander (cilantro) including
   roots, stems and leaves
2 teaspoons palm sugar
1 tablespoon light soy sauce
2 tablespoons evaporated milk

SERVES 4

Method

MARINADE
Pound the garlic and salt with a mortar and pestle then add the peppercorns and coriander. Pound again until the ingredients are well combined. Lightly pound in the sugar then add all of the remaining ingredients and mix well.

Transfer the marinade to a large bowl. Add the chicken pieces and mix until well coated with the marinade. Marinate for at least 1 hour.

GRILLING
Thread each piece of chicken onto a skewer to keep the chicken as flat as possible.
Grill (broil) over hot coals for about 20 minutes, or until cooked, turning a few times.
Alternatively, oven roast at 180°C/350°F/Gas mark 4 for about 1 hour, or until cooked.

Kaeng Matsaman Muu [Massaman Pork Curry]

Kaeng Matsaman, literally translates as 'Muslim' curry, and is a popular southern Thai curry, which is largely influenced by Indian or Malay flavours. Of course, practising Muslims never eat pork so they would never eat this type of Massaman curry, which also comes in beef or chicken versions (see recipe). The addition of coconut cream, potatoes and peanuts results in a smooth yet mildly spicy curry.

Ingredients

3 cups (1¼ pint/750 ml) coconut cream
3 tablespoons Massaman Curry Paste
   (*see* recipe)
14 oz (400 g) pork, cut into ¾ in
   (2 cm) dice
1½ tablespoons tamarind pulp
5 cardamom pods, toasted in a dry pan
   until fragrant
1¾ in (4 cm) cinnamon quill (stick),
   toasted in a dry pan until fragrant
½ teaspoon salt
2 large or 3 medium potatoes, cut into
   ¾ in (2 cm) dice
3 shallot segments (about
   1½ tablespoons), sliced
3 teaspoons fish sauce (nam pla)
1½ tablespoons Thai palm sugar
2 tablespoons unsalted roasted peanuts

To Serve
Steamed jasmine rice

Serves 3–4

Method

Make tamarind liquid by soaking 2 teaspoons tamarind pulp in 1½ tablespoons hot water. Stir and strain it when cool and set aside.

Put ½ cup (4 fl oz/125 ml) of the coconut cream into a cold pan or wok and cook over medium heat for 2–3 minutes, or until the oil separates and rises to the surface.

Add the Massaman Curry Paste. Turn the heat to medium-low and fry, stirring, for about 2 minutes or until aromatic. Add the pork and stir to coat with curry paste. Add the toasted cardamom pods and cinnamon and fry until the pork changes colour.

Now add the remaining coconut cream and salt. Bring to the boil then reduce the heat to low and simmer, uncovered, for 1½–2 hours, stirring occasionally. Add the potatoes, shallots, fish sauce, tamarind, palm sugar and peanuts and continue to simmer for another 30 minutes or until the potatoes are cooked.

Serve with steamed jasmine rice.

> **Alternatives & Variations**
> • Use onion instead of shallots.
> • Use brown sugar instead of palm sugar.
> • Use beef or chicken instead of pork. Reduce the cooking time for chicken.

Kiaw [Wontons]

Wontons are dumplings filled with meat and spices. Often they are served in soup.

Ingredients

1 lb 2 oz (500 g) pork mince
1 heaped tablespoon white (granulated) sugar
1 teaspoon white pepper
1 small egg
2 teaspoons light soy sauce
1 teaspoon Thai seasoning sauce
1 packet thin wonton wrappers

MAKES ABOUT 60 SMALL OR 40 LARGER WONTONS

Method

Put the pork mince on a chopping board and, using a cleaver or very sharp knife, quickly chop the mince back and forth several times. Turn it over and repeat.

Place in a bowl with the sugar, pepper, egg, soy sauce and seasoning sauce. Mix until very well combined and the mixture is smooth. Cover and place in the coldest part of the refrigerator for at least 2 hours, or place in the freezer until starting to freeze.

Place a wonton wrapper on the palm of your hand. Scrape a teaspoon-sized piece of mince into the middle of the wrapper. Gather the edges together and squeeze gently above the mixture with your fingertips to make a small pouch. Repeat with remaining mixture and wrappers.

When you are ready to cook the wontons, bring a large pan of water to the boil. Add the desired number of wontons, reduce the heat and simmer for about 3 minutes, or until they float to the surface.

Note: Wontons can be frozen uncooked for up to 3 months. Freeze on a tray, then transfer to a container.

Alternatives & Variations
- Other seasoning sauces can be used in the wontons but tend to have a stronger flavour than Thai seasoning sauce. Use sparingly, or use extra light soy sauce instead.
- Make the wonton mixture in a food processor. Process the pork first then add the remaining ingredients.

Khai Yat Sai [Thai Omelette with Minced Pork]

The Thai omelette is traditionally fried in a lot of oil, which makes it quite puffy. The following recipe is one that I developed after watching many Thai omelettes being cooked. I use a small amount of oil but you could use more if you want that puffiness. It is difficult to cook more than one omelette at a time.

Ingredients

2 eggs
2 thin onion slices (about 1 tablespoon)
2 tablespoons tomato, chopped
1 tablespoon garlic chives, finely chopped
½ teaspoon fish sauce (nam pla)
¼ teaspoon lime juice
White pepper, to taste
2 teaspoons peanut oil
½ teaspoon garlic, peeled and finely
    chopped
1 tablespoon minced pork

TO SERVE
Plain rice
Sweet chilli sauce

SERVES 1 OR 2

Method

Crack the eggs into a small bowl. Add the onion, tomato, garlic chives, fish sauce, lime juice and pepper. Beat lightly with a fork.

Heat the wok over high heat and add the oil. Add the garlic and pork and stir-fry for about 15–20 seconds until the pork is cooked.

Pour in the egg mixture and gently spread it around the base of the wok. Reduce the heat to medium-high and cook for 1 minute. Turn it over and cook for another minute (you may need to break it into 2 or 3 sections to do so).

Serve on a bed of plain rice and drizzle with sweet chilli sauce or serve with the sauce on the side.

Alternatives & Variations
• Use lemon juice instead of lime juice.
• For a vegetarian omelette, simply omit the pork.

Yam Neua [Thai Beef Salad]

This dish is a good example of how important presentation is in Thai cooking; the salad ingredients need to be prepared with great care and precision. The flavours in this dish can be adjusted according to personal taste: you can change the heat by altering the number of chillies, the saltiness by the amount of fish sauce, the sourness by the amount of lime juice, and the sweetness by the amount of sugar.

Ingredients

1 teaspoon peanut oil
1 teaspoon garlic, minced (crushed)
5 oz (150 g) beef fillet, thinly sliced
1 tablespoon fish sauce (nam pla)
1½ tablespoons lime juice
1 teaspoon sugar
½ teaspoon vinegar from a jar of pickled garlic (available from Asian food stores)
1 small or ½ large tomato, sliced into thin wedges
¼ cup (1¼ oz/35 g) onion, thinly sliced lengthways
2–2¼ in (5–6 cm) piece cucumber, peeled, quartered lengthways then sliced diagonally
5 bird's eye chillies, red or green or mixed, thinly sliced

Garnish
Lettuce leaves
½ tablespoon coriander (cilantro) leaves
½ tablespoon garlic chives, cut into 1¼ in (3 cm) lengths

Serves 2 as an appetiser or as one dish in a shared meal

Method

Heat the wok to medium hot and add the oil. Add the garlic, stir for a few seconds and add the beef. Increase the heat to high and stir-fry for about 2 minutes, or until cooked to your liking. Remove to a bowl and set aside to cool.

Once the beef is cold, add the fish sauce, lime juice, sugar and vinegar. Mix well to coat the beef. Add the vegetables and toss until combined. Taste and adjust the flavours if necessary.

Serve on a bed of lettuce and garnish with coriander and garlic chives.

Alternatives & Variations
- Lemon juice can be substituted for lime juice.
- Use white vinegar instead of pickled garlic vinegar.
- Ordinary chives or the tops of spring onions can be used instead of garlic chives.

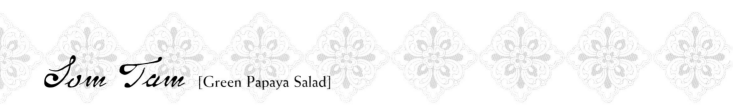

Som Tam [Green Papaya Salad]

This is one of the most popular Thai salads in Thailand. As with Thai Beef Salad, the flavours in this dish can be adjusted according to personal taste: you can change the heat by the number of chillies, the saltiness by the amount of fish sauce, the sourness by the amount of lime juice and the sweetness by the amount of sugar. Usually these spicy dishes are served with something quite bland such as raw beans, white cabbage or sticky (glutinous) rice. It is delicious and refreshing on a warm summer's day.

Ingredients

1 small or ½ large green papaya, shredded
2 red bird's eye chillies
2 small garlic cloves
1 oz (30 g) unsalted roasted peanuts
½–1 tablespoon whole dried shrimp (prawn)
1 tablespoon Thai palm sugar, softened in the microwave, if necessary
1½ tablespoons lime juice
1 tablespoon fish sauce (nam pla)
2 snake beans, cut into 2–3 cm (¾–1¼ in) lengths

To Serve
Raw white cabbage leaves, torn into large pieces
Raw green beans, topped and tailed

Serves 2 as a side dish

Method

Peel the skin off half of the papaya, wash it and dry with paper towels. Holding the unpeeled half and using a large, sharp knife or cleaver, quickly chop the peeled half back and forth vertically until the surface is very well scored.

Now thinly slice lengthways and away from you to cut shreds of papaya. Continue scoring and slicing until you have enough shredded papaya, peeling the other half if needed.

Pound the chillies and garlic in a large mortar and pestle or crush the garlic, finely chop the chillies and place in a large bowl.

Add the peanuts, dried shrimp, palm sugar, lime juice, fish sauce and beans. Lightly pound with the pestle or a wooden spoon until combined.

Add the shredded papaya to the mortar and lightly pound or mix again to combine the papaya with the other ingredients. If you only have a smaller mortar and pestle, use it to pound the other ingredients then transfer to a large bowl before adding the papaya. Serve immediately with the white cabbage and beans.

> Alternatives & Variations
> • Lemon juice can be substituted for lime juice.
> • Use 6 green beans instead of snake beans. If large, cut in half lengthways.
> • Cucumber can be substituted for green papaya. Be careful when shredding.
> • Soft brown sugar or Indonesian palm sugar can be used instead of Thai palm sugar.

Tao-Huu Phat Thua Ngawk [Fried Tofu with Beansprouts]

Tofu (also called beancurd) is widely used in Thailand. Blocks of fresh tofu can be kept in the refrigerator for several days providing it is covered with water and the water is changed daily.

Ingredients

1 tablespoon oyster sauce
1½ teaspoons light soy sauce
½ teaspoon fish sauce (nam pla)
1 teaspoon sugar
1 cup (8 fl oz/250 ml) vegetable oil
3 cups (1½ lb/675 g) fresh tofu, cut into
　　¾ in (2 cm) dice
1 teaspoon garlic, minced (crushed)
2 large handfuls beansprouts
½ cup garlic chives, cut into 2 in (5 cm)
　　lengths
½ teaspoon chicken seasoning powder
　　(optional)

SERVES 4

Method

For convenience combine the sauces and sugar in a small bowl before you start.

Heat the oil in a wok over medium-high heat. When hot, add the tofu and fry until golden brown. Stir and turn the tofu as it fries. The frying time depends on the type of tofu used, but it should take about 1–2 minutes.

Now carefully pour off all but about 1 tablespoon of oil. Push the tofu to one side of the wok, add the garlic and fry, stirring for 10 seconds. Then mix with the tofu.

Toss in the beansprouts, garlic chives, sugar, sauces and chicken seasoning powder (if using). Stir-fry for 30 seconds until well combined.

Alternatives & Variations
• Spring onion (scallion) tops or ordinary chives can be used instead of garlic chives.

# Thak Kaat Dong [Pickled Cabbage]

Pickled cabbage is mainly used with noodle soups. It can be chopped and added or served as an accompaniment. It goes perfectly with the Chiang Mai Chicken Curry Noodles (Khao Soi).

Ingredients

9 oz (250 g) white cabbage
1 cup (4 fl oz/120 ml) rice vinegar
¼ cup (1¾ oz/50 g) sugar
½ tablespoon salt

MAKES ABOUT 2 CUPS

Method

Separate the cabbages leaves, place in a large bowl and leave in a warm place for 24 hours until wilted.

Place the rice vinegar, sugar and salt in a small pan over low heat and stir until the sugar dissolves. Increase the heat and bring to the boil, then allow to cool.

Cut the cabbage into smaller chunks and pack into a sterilised preserving jar. Pour the cooled vinegar over, seal and leave for a few days before using.

Refrigerate after opening and use within 2–3 weeks.

Pad Thai [Thai Fried Noodles]

Pad Thai is one of the simplest Thai dishes and one of the most delicious. It is important to serve Pad Thai with wedges of lime and dried chilli flakes. For a truly authentic version, serve with the traditional Thai condiments.

Ingredients

3½ oz (100 g) thin flat dried rice noodles
1 tablespoon fish sauce (nam pla)
½ teaspoon Thai seasoning sauce
2 teaspoons chilli sauce
2 teaspoons tamarind liquid or paste
1½ tablespoons sugar
2 teaspoons peanut or vegetable oil
1 tablespoon whole dried shrimp
2 eggs
2 large handfuls fresh beansprouts
½ cup (1¾ oz/50 g) spring onions
   (scallions) or garlic chives, cut into
   4 cm (1¾ in) lengths
2–3 tablespoons unsalted roasted
   peanuts, finely crushed

ACCOMPANIMENTS
½ lime, cut in half
5 slices peeled cucumber, cut in half
2 whole spring onions (scallions) or garlic
   chives

PHRIK NAAM PLAA
Red and green birds eye chillies
fish sauce (nam pla)

NAAM SOM PHRIKV
Long green chillies
White vinegar

THAI CONDIMENTS
Small bowls of white sugar
Dried chillies flakes
Phrik Naam Plaa (*see* above)
Naam Som Phrik (*see* above)

SERVES 2

Method

Soak the noodles in cold water for 2½–3 hours until they are slightly softened. Alternatively, soak in hot water for about 10 minutes. (Use the cold water method the first time you make this dish to get an idea of the required consistency. If the noodles are too soft before stir-frying you will end up with soggy Pad Thai.)

Mix the sauces and sugar together in a small bowl.

Heat the wok over medium heat and add the oil. Add the dried shrimp and fry, stirring for 10 seconds. Break in the eggs, mix lightly with the shrimp and gently spread around the base of the wok. Cook for 10 seconds then turn over, break up a little and cook for another 15 seconds.

Reduce heat to medium-low. Drain the noodles very briefly and toss into the wok. They should be wet. Now add the sauce and sugar mixture. Increase the heat to high and stir-fry for 1 minute until well combined.

Add the beansprouts and the spring onions or garlic chive lengths. Stir-fry for 30–60 seconds, or until well combined with the noodles then turn off the heat.

Place the noodles on a serving dish. Scatter the peanuts on top and place the accompaniments on the side of the plate.

PHRIK NAAM PLAA [FISH SAUCE WITH SLICED BIRDS EYE CHILLIES]
Thinly slice some red and green birds eye chillies. Place in a small bowl with some good quality fish sauce.

NAAM SOM PHRIK [GREEN CHILLIES IN VINEGAR]
Thinly slice some long green chillies and place in a small dish with some white vinegar..

> **Alternatives & Variations**
> • Instead of dried shrimp, use fresh shrimp (prawns), sliced squid, chicken or shredded white cabbage. Stir-fry until cooked before adding the eggs.
> • Add a small handful of deep-fried cubed tofu and/or 1 teaspoon finely chopped salted radish.
> • Use 2 teaspoons light soy sauce instead of Thai seasoning sauce.

Phat Khao Kai Phak [Thai Fried Rice with Chicken and Vegetables]

Thai fried rice is characteristically very peppery so you can reduce the amount of pepper to suit your palate.

Ingredients

2 teaspoons oyster sauce

1 teaspoon light soy sauce

½ teaspoon Thai seasoning sauce

¼ teaspoon dark soy sauce

1 teaspoon sugar

¼ teaspoon white pepper or less

1 teaspoon vegetable oil

¼ teaspoon garlic, minced

3½ oz (100 g chicken thigh or breast fillet, thinly sliced

1 egg

2 cups (14 oz/400 g) cooked rice, hot or cold

½ cup (2 oz/60 g) white cabbage, shredded

¼ cup (½ oz/15 g)carrot, julienned

¼ cup (2 oz/60 g) onion, thinly sliced lengthways

1 small or ½ large tomato, sliced into thin wedges

¼–½ cup garlic chives, cut into ¾ in (2 cm) lengths

SERVES 2 OR AS ONE DISH IN A
SHARED MEAL

Method

Mix the sauces, sugar and pepper into a small bowl.

Heat the wok over high heat and add the oil. Add the garlic and fry for 5 seconds before adding the chicken. Stir-fry over high heat until the chicken turns white.

Crack in the egg and move it gently around the wok for a few seconds before mixing it with the chicken.

Add the rice and stir-fry for 30 seconds (if using cold rice, stir-fry for 2–3 minutes until hot). Then add the cabbage, carrot, onion and tomato and cook for 1 minute.

Add the combined sauces, sugar and pepper and stir-fry until well combined.

Add the garlic chives, turn off the heat, mix through and serve.

Alternatives & Variations
- Ordinary chives or the tops of spring onions can be used instead of garlic chives.
- Use extra light soy sauce or fish sauce instead of Thai seasoning sauce.
- Use leftover rice up to 2 days old.
- Use pork or seafood instead of chicken.
- For vegetarian fried rice, omit the chicken. Add extra vegetables of your choice and another egg.

Kuaytiaw Haeng Sukhothai

[Seasoned Rice Noodles with Barbecue Pork, Peanuts, Green Beans and Beansprouts]

The list of ingredients may seem long but the dish is very easy to put together. There is also a soup version of this dish known as Kuaytiaw Naam Tom Yum. In addition, the ingredients such as barbecue pork (Char Siew), Pork Gravy and Crispy Fried Garlic are used in many other Asian recipes.

Ingredients

3½ oz (100 g) thin flat rice noodles, soaked in hot water for 10 minutes, drained and put aside

½ cup (2½ oz/75 g) green (French) beans, sliced diagonally

3 teaspoons Crispy Fried Garlic (*see recipe*)

1 teaspoon fish sauce (nam pla)

3 teaspoons Thai palm sugar, softened for a few seconds in the microwave, if necessary

3 teaspoons Pork Gravy (*see recipe*)

1 teaspoon lime juice

12 slices Char Siew (barbecue pork, *see recipe*)

1 teaspoon salted radish, chopped

2 tablespoons unsalted roasted peanuts, finely crushed

2 tablespoons coriander (cilantro) leaves and stems, finely chopped

2 tablespoons spring onions (scallions), finely chopped

1–2 teaspoons dried chilli flakes, or to taste

1 cup (3½ oz/100 g) fresh beansprouts

6 pieces crispy pork crackling

SERVES 2

Method

Bring a large pan of water to the boil. Add the noodles and beans, reduce the heat to medium and cook for 1 minute. Drain and divide between 2 serving bowls. Divide the Crispy Fried Garlic, fish sauce, palm sugar, Pork Gravy and lime juice between the bowls. Toss well with chopsticks to coat the noodles and mix the ingredients.

Scatter each bowl with half of the barbecue pork slices, salted radish, peanuts, coriander and spring onions. Place the dried chilli flakes, beansprouts and pork crackling in small heaps on the side of each bowl.

Alternatives & Variations
- There is no alternative for salted radish but it can be omitted without making too much difference.
- Use prepared barbecue pork (char siew), available from some Chinese barbecue restaurants. Ask for some gravy!

Khrevang Kaeng Khiaw Waan [Green Curry Paste]

This green curry paste can be made in a food processor or blender, although most Thai cooks believe that a better result is obtained by using a mortar and pestle. Make this curry paste when you have some extra hands available to take turns and make easier work of the pounding!

Ingredients

1 cardamom pod
2 teaspoons coriander seeds
½ teaspoon cumin seeds
³/₈ in (1 cm) piece prok hom or dried kencur (optional; include only if the curry paste is to be used with chicken)
1 tablespoon garlic cloves
3 stalks lemongrass, roughly sliced
¼ cup coriander (cilantro) leaves and stems
3 coriander roots, cut into 3 or 4 pieces
1 tablespoon fresh galangal, roughly chopped
2 tablespoons green bird's eye chillies
4 red bird's eye chillies
½ teaspoon salt
1 tablespoon garlic cloves (extra), finely chopped
1 teaspoon Thai shrimp paste

MAKES ABOUT ½ CUP (4 FL OZ/125 ML) CURRY PASTE

Method

Toast the cardamom pod, coriander and cumin seeds separately in a dry wok or pan, stirring over medium-low heat for about 3 minutes until aromatic. Transfer to a mortar, allow to cool, then add the prok hom and grind to a fine powder.

Place all the other ingredients except for the salt, extra garlic and shrimp paste in a food processor and chop finely. Add the chopped ingredients to the ground ingredients in the mortar, add the salt and pound until you have a thick paste. Have a spatula ready to scrape down the sides of the mortar and to stop the paste escaping.

Add the extra garlic and continue to pound until the curry paste is well combined and comes together. This will take about 20–30 minutes.

Add the shrimp paste and pound until blended. Stored in an airtight jar in the refrigerator for up to 1 month or freeze in portions.

Alternatives & Variations
• If fresh galangal is not available, use half the quantity of fresh ginger root. The flavour will be slightly different but still delicious.
• For a milder curry, remove the seeds from the bird's eye chillies or substitute 5 or 6 large green chillies.
• Use Indonesian or Malaysian shrimp paste instead of Thai.
• Make the curry paste in a food processor or electric blender. Add the ingredients in the same order and add 1–3 tablespoons of water to assist blending.
• Make a double or triple quantity and freeze to have a ready supply of curry paste so that delicious green curries can be made in minutes.

Khreuang Kaeng Phet [Red Curry Paste]

Red curry paste is one of the most versatile Thai curry pastes. It is used in several other dishes in addition to the classic red curry. Try using it in Thai fish cakes or stir-fries.

Ingredients

20 large dried red chillies, roughly chopped, about 1¾ oz (50 g)

1½ tablespoons fresh galangal, roughly sliced

2 tablespoons garlic cloves (about 8 cloves)

3 stalks lemongrass, roughly sliced

3 coriander (cilantro) roots, cut into 3 or 4 pieces

2 tablespoons garlic cloves, extra

5 fresh red bird's eye chillies

5 fresh green bird's eye chillies

1 teaspoons salt

2 teaspoons Thai shrimp paste

MAKES ABOUT 1½ CUPS (12 FL OZ/ 350 ML) CURRY PASTE

Method

Place the first 5 ingredients in a food processor and finely chop. Transfer to a mortar.

Finely chop the extra garlic and fresh chillies (by hand or in the food processor) and add to the mortar with the salt. Pound until you have a thick, slightly wet paste.

Hold a spatula or large spoon in your other hand and use to scrape down the sides of the mortar and to stop the paste escaping.

Add the shrimp paste and pound until well combined.

Store in an airtight jar in the refrigerator for up to 1 month or freeze in portions.

Alternatives & Variations

- If fresh galangal is not available, use half the quantity of fresh ginger, which has a similar, but stronger flavour.
- For a milder curry paste, remove the seeds from the chillies.
- Use Indonesian or Malaysian shrimp paste instead of Thai paste so that delicious green curries can be made in minutes.
- Make the curry paste in a food processor or electric blender. Add the ingredients in the same order and add 1–2 tablespoons of water if necessary to assist blending.
- Make a double or triple quantity and freeze to have a ready supply of curry paste so that delicious red curries can be made in minutes.

Khruang Matsaman [Massaman Curry Paste]

This mild curry paste draws on the flavours originally brought to Thailand by Muslim traders, hence the name Massaman (Muslim).

Ingredients

1½ tablespoons coriander seeds
1 tablespoon lemongrass, finely sliced
1 teaspoon cumin seeds
½ tablespoon galangal, finely chopped
5 medium shallot segments, peeled
3 large garlic cloves, peeled
4 large dried red chillies, seeded and split
   open lengthways
¼ teaspoon black peppercorns
1 teaspoon salt
½ tablespoon Thai shrimp paste

MAKES ABOUT 3 TABLESPOONS

Method

In a dry pan or wok over medium-low heat, toast the coriander seeds, lemongrass, cumin seeds and galangal. Toast for 3–5 minutes or until aromatic, stirring or shaking frequently to prevent burning. Transfer to a mortar or spice grinder.

Add the shallots and the garlic to the pan and toast for 2–3 minutes, or until lightly browned. Set aside.

Toast the dried chillies, pressing lightly and turning frequently for about 2 minutes, or until well toasted. Cool slightly then roughly chop with a pair of scissors.

Grind the coriander seeds, lemongrass, cumin seeds, galangal and peppercorns finely, add the shallots, garlic and salt and grind again. Now add the chillies and continue to grind until you have a thick paste. Add the shrimp paste and grind again until well combined. Makes about 3 tablespoons of curry paste.

Note: This curry paste can be stored in an airtight jar in the refrigerator for up to 1 month or can be frozen in portions.

> Alternatives & Variations
> • Use fresh ginger instead of galangal.
> • Use Indonesian or Malaysian shrimp paste instead of Thai.
> • Use onion instead of shallots.
> • Make the curry paste in a food processor or electric blender.
> • Make a double or triple quantity of curry paste to freeze.

Kratiam Thawt [Crispy Fried Garlic]

Crispy Fried Garlic is widely used throughout Thailand as a sauce or garnish and is a popular addition to a bowl of soup or noodles. It keeps well in an airtight jar so it is worthwhile making a couple of months' supply.

Ingredients

½ cup (4 fl oz/125 ml) peanut or
   vegetable oil
2 heads or 20 garlic cloves, peeled and
   coarsely minced (crushed)

MAKES ABOUT ½ CUP (4 FL OZ/125 ML)

Method

Heat the oil in a small pan over medium-low heat and fry the garlic in 2 batches, stirring constantly for about 4–6 minutes, or until light golden. The oil should not be too hot or the garlic will brown too quickly.

Remove the garlic from the oil and place in a screw-top glass jar.

After frying the final batch of garlic, allow the oil to cool slightly and pour enough into the jar to cover the garlic. Can be stored in a cool, dark place for up to 2 months.

Alternatives & Variations
• Packaged Crispy Fried Garlic can be purchased from Asian food stores (in plastic jars or packets) and is a satisfactory substitute.

Khanom Farang [Egg Cakes]

Sweet, light and airy, these egg cakes are served as a dessert.

Ingredients

2 eggs
3½ oz (100 g) caster (superfine) sugar
4 tablespoons self-raising (self-rising)
   flour, sifted 3 times

MAKES 24

Method

Preheat the oven to 180°C/350°F/Gas mark 4. Lightly grease two 12-hole patty tins (pans).

Beat the eggs and sugar in a small bowl until pale, thick and frothy. This will take about 5 minutes with an electric mixer on high speed. Transfer the mixture to a larger bowl and lightly fold in the sifted flour.

Use to half fill the patty tins and bake for about 6 minutes, or until golden and crisp around the edges. Stand for a few minutes before removing from tins.

Naam Phrik Pao [Fried Dried Chilli, Garlic, Shallot and Shrimp Paste Sauce]

This sauce is particularly good with the north-eastern Thai grilled chicken dish called Kai Yaang (see recipe). It can also be used as a dip with raw vegetables or a spoonful added to Tom Yam Soup (see recipe) to give it that deep red colour and extra flavour.

Ingredients

¼ cup (2 fl oz/60 ml) peanut oil
¼ cup garlic cloves, thinly sliced
¼ cup shallot segments, thinly sliced
¼ cup large red dried chillies, seeded and
    roughly chopped
1½ tablespoons palm sugar
½ teaspoon salt
2 teaspoons Thai shrimp paste
2 teaspoons fish sauce (nam pla)

MAKES ABOUT ½ CUP (4 FL OZ/125 ML)

Method

Heat the oil in a wok over medium heat. Add the garlic and fry for about 2 minutes until golden. Drain and place in a mortar or small food processor.

Repeat with the shallots, frying until dark golden and slightly crisp.

Fry the chillies for a few seconds until crisp and dark in colour. Drain and add to the garlic and shallots. Turn off the heat.

Pound or process the garlic, shallots and chillies to a smooth paste.

Reheat the oil over medium-low heat, add the paste, palm sugar, salt and shrimp paste and fry for about 1 minute until thick and oily. Add the fish sauce and fry for another 30 seconds.

Cool and store in a jar in the refrigerator. It will keep for several weeks.

Alternatives & Variations
• Use brown sugar instead of palm sugar.

Khao Niaw Ma-Muang

[Sweet Sticky Rice with Mango and Coconut Cream]

This is a very popular sweet snack in Thailand during the mango season. The crispy mung beans add a delicious crunch.

Ingredients

2 cups (14 oz/400 g) sticky (glutinous) rice, soaked overnight in plenty of cold water

½ cup (4 fl oz/125 ml) coconut milk

¼ cup (3½ oz/100 g) sugar, plus 1 tablespoon extra

Pinch of salt

½ cup (4 fl oz/125 ml) coconut cream

1 large or 2 small mangoes

CRISPY MUNG BEANS

2 tablespoons green mung beans, soaked overnight in cold water

2 tablespoons vegetable oil

SERVES 4

Method

CRISPY MUNG BEANS

Drain the beans and place in a large bowl. Rub handfuls between your palms to remove the skins. Fill the bowl with water and slowly pour if off. The skins will float out of the bowl. Spread on paper towels to dry.

Heat the oil in a pan over medium heat. Add the beans and fry for about 1 minute until lightly coloured. Drain on paper towels and cool before using.

STICKY RICE

Drain and rinse the rice. Line a steamer with muslin; place the rice inside in an even layer and steam over medium-high heat for 40 minutes. Add extra boiling water to the pan if necessary. Place the cooked rice in a bowl.

Combine the coconut milk, ¼ cup (2 fl oz/60 ml) sugar and salt and pour over the hot rice. Fold it through and leave to cool. Mix the coconut cream and extra sugar and set aside.

When ready to serve, place a mound of rice in each bowl, top with slices of mango and pour over the reserved coconut cream mixture.Add the Crispy Mung Beans in a small pile to the side of the bowl.

Malaysia and Singapore

Malaysia and Singapore — Introduction

Malaysia and Singapore's multicultural societies are responsible for the fabulous variety in their cuisines. The majority of each of their populations consists of a harmonious mixture of Malays, Chinese and Indians, and their different styles of cuisines also complement each other.

It is wonderful to see Indian families enjoying a Chinese dim sum meal and Chinese families having an Indian feast. Eating in Malaysia and Singapore is a very enjoyable experience and never, ever boring. In Malaysia, night markets are set up every evening in almost every town while Singapore is famous for its hawker food centres with their amazing selection of foods on offer.

While truly indigenous Malay dishes such as Nasi Lemak (coconut rice with boiled egg, crispy fried anchovies and peanuts and spicy sambal) do exist, one of the most interesting cuisines in Malaysia comes from two combined cuisines. Nonya cuisine (also called Peranakan or Straits Chinese cuisine) is a result of the intermarriage between Chinese men (Baba) and Malay women (Nonya). Nonya dishes, such as Laksa (a spicy, coconut milk–based noodle soup) and Ayam Buah Keras (chicken cooked in a candle nut and spice paste) combine Chinese methods and ingredients with fragrant and spicy Malaysian ingredients such as chillies, lemongrass, turmeric, lime leaves, shrimp paste and coconut milk. However, not all Nonya dishes are spicy. Ayam Pong Teh (chicken with soybean paste, potatoes and mushrooms) and Bak Siou (pork ribs simmered in a ground coriander, vinegar and palm sugar paste) are good examples of milder dishes.

Chinese food can be found all over Malaysia and Singapore but the largest concentration of Chinese people in Malaysia is found on Penang Island. Here you will find all of the Chinese regional specialities with fantastic dim sum (small serves of delicious steamed or fried dumplings, buns, meat and seafood called tim sum in Penang) served morning, noon and night. You will also find Chinese barbecued pork and duck as well as the famous Hainan steamed or roasted chicken rice and Char Koay Teow (stir-fried flat rice noodles) to name but a few. Perhaps the most famous Singaporean dish is the deliciously spicy Singapore chilli crab.

Indian food too is very well represented in Malaysia with an enormous variety to choose from. Malaysia's nasi kandar restaurants offer a huge selection of Indian curries, breads, tandoori dishes and lassis. Nasi kandar is a meal of rice served with other dishes such as curries, which was traditionally sold by street vendors from a yoke over their shoulders. A Malay/Indian breakfast speciality is Roti Canai, a flaky fried flatbread that is served with a small dish of curry sauce, often coconut milk–based. These breads are usually made at the front of the restaurant and it's a joy to watch the chefs throw and slap the dough until it is paper-thin and then twist it into a coil, press it flat and fry it on a huge hotplate.

When I'm in Malaysia my favourite meal is breakfast where I rotate between three favourites. One day it's Malaysian nasi lemak, the next it's Chinese dim sum and the third it's Indian roti canai! In the following pages you will find recipes from all four cuisines, so you can either have a meal with a single theme or a multicultural feast!

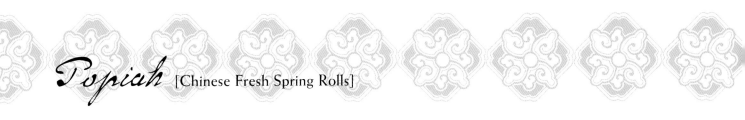

Popiah [Chinese Fresh Spring Rolls]

These delicious snacks can be found at specialist food stalls throughout Singapore and Malaysia. They are a little fiddly to make but worthwhile. All of the components can be made in advance and the Popiah can be rolled just before serving or set out on a platter for everyone to roll their own. They are a deliciously healthy alternative to fried spring rolls. You can use daikon radish plus 1 teaspoon sugar if yam bean is not available.

Ingredients

6 teaspoons sweet soy sauce (kecap manis)
3–6 teaspoons Fried Chilli Paste (*see* recipe)
1 large garlic clove, minced
2 hard-boiled eggs, finely chopped
½ cup seafood cocktail, finely chopped
1 cup (3½ oz/100 g) beansprouts
2¾ in (8 cm) piece cucumber, peeled, deseeded and coarsely grated
3 small lettuce leaves, halved
2 tablespoons crisp fried wonton wrappers, coarsely crushed
12 tablespoons filling (*see* opposite)
3 tablespoons unsalted roasted peanuts, finely crushed

CRÊPES
1 egg, beaten
½ cup (4 fl oz/125 ml) water or milk, plus extra, if needed
½ cup (2 oz/ 60 g) plain (all-purpose) flour
1 large pinch salt
1 tablespoon oil

Method

CRÊPES
Beat all the ingredients to a thin batter. Set aside for at least 20 minutes.

Meanwhile, make the filling. Heat a wok or pan over medium-low heat and add the oil. Add the garlic, ginger and shallots and fry for 30 seconds.

Add the grated turnip and sauté for 4 minutes.

Add the remaining ingredients, reduce the heat to low, cover and simmer for another 4 minutes. Keep covered until ready to use.

Beat the batter again before cooking and add a little extra water if it has thickened.

Using a non-stick frying-pan, pour in enough batter to barely cover the base. Cook until dry on top and remove. Repeat to make 12 medium crêpes.

Filling

2 teaspoons peanut oil

1 garlic clove, peeled and finely chopped

1 teaspoon fresh ginger, finely chopped

2 shallot segments (about 1 tablespoon), sliced

1 medium sweet turnip (yam bean), grated (shredded)

2 tablespoons Chicken Stock (*see* recipe)

1 teaspoon vinegar

2 large pinches salt

Makes 6 large rolls

Assembling

Arrange 2 crêpes flat on a board slightly overlapping each other by about a quarter (like Olympic rings).

Place 1 teaspoon soy sauce, ½–1 teaspoon chilli paste and ¼ teaspoon minced garlic in the middle and spread out using the back of a spoon.

Place 2 teaspoons egg, 1 teaspoon seafood cocktail, a few beansprouts, ½ tablespoon cucumber, ½ lettuce leaf, 1 teaspoon crispy wonton and 2 tablespoons of sweet turnip mixture across the middle of the crêpes, leaving at least 2 in (5 cm) on each side. Top with 2 teaspoons of crushed peanuts.

Fold the 2 sides of the crêpes to cover the filling then fold the base up and roll firmly. Place on a tray while making the remaining Popiah.

Cut each into 4 or 5 pieces. Alternatively, serve all of the ingredients on a large platter or in bowls and allow people to roll their own.

Otak-Otak [Fragrant Fish Paste Parcels Wrapped in Banana Leaves]

These deliciously fragrant and spicy little fish parcels can be found grilling (broiling) over charcoal in many Malaysian night markets.

Ingredients

1 lb 6 oz (600 g) white fish fillets, minced
6 kaffir lime leaves, finely shredded
1 teaspoon salt
⅓ cup (2¼ oz/65 g) caster (superfine) sugar
1 egg
20 x 6 in (15 cm) squares banana leaf or foil
Small bamboo sticks or bamboo skewers quartered, then split into 3 or 4 pieces

Spice Paste

1 tablespoon coriander seeds, dry-fried for 5 minutes over low heat
4–6 large dried red chillies, seeded and soaked in hot water for 15 minutes
2¼ in (6 cm) piece fresh ginger, roughly chopped
1 tablespoon turmeric root, roughly chopped
10 shallot segments, roughly chopped
1 stalk lemongrass (bottom white section), roughly sliced
5 candle nuts, roughly chopped
1 teaspoon shrimp paste
3 tablespoons oil
1¼ cups (10 fl oz/625 ml) coconut cream

Serves 4 (20 parcels)

Method

To make the filling, mix the minced fish, kaffir lime leaves, salt and sugar together in a bowl. Set aside, covered.

Spice Paste

Meanwhile, grind the coriander seeds to a powder in a mortar or small food processor. Drain the dried chillies, add to the coriander and grind to a paste. Gradually add the ginger, turmeric, shallots, lemongrass and candle nuts and continue to pound until evenly coloured and fairly smooth (if using a food processor add these ingredients all together). Finally work in the shrimp paste.

Heat a wok or pan over low heat and add the oil.

Add the spice paste, increase the heat to medium-low and fry, stirring almost constantly for about 10 minutes, or until the oil starts to separate. Add the coconut cream and stir well. Cool for a few minutes before using.

Fish Parcels

Add the warm spice paste to the fish mixture along with the egg. Mix well until you have a thick smooth paste.

Place about 2 tablespoons of the paste along the bottom third of a square of banana leaf or foil. Roll up and secure the ends with small bamboo sticks (if using foil, fold the ends to secure).

Cook over hot coals, under a grill (broiler) or in a hot oven for about 15 minutes or until firm.

Alternatives & Variations
• Use 1 teaspoon finely grated lime rind instead of kaffir lime leaves.
• Use 5 macadamia nuts or 10 blanched almonds instead of candle nuts.

Penang Prawn Mee [Spicy Shrimp and Egg Noodle Soup]

This soup is perfect fodder for spicy food lovers! The preparation can be time-consuming but, as with many other Asian soups, most ingredients can be prepared well ahead of time and put together when ready to serve.

Ingredients

3 cups (1¼ pints/750 ml) Spicy Shrimp Broth (*see* below)
2 cups (10 oz/280 g) fresh egg noodles, loosely packed
2 small handfuls beansprouts
2 small handfuls kangkung or Asian greens, sliced into 2 in (5 cm) pieces
1 boiled egg, sliced
1 fish cake, sliced
8 slices cooked pork (optional)
Cooked shrimp from the Spicy Prawn Broth (*see* below)

Spicy Shrimp Broth
8 raw jumbo shrimp (king prawns), shelled, but keep the shells and leave the tail intact)
2 cups (16 fl oz/500 ml) water
½ teaspoon salt, plus extra to taste
3 cups (1¼ pints/750 ml) Chicken Stock (*see* recipe)
1 tablespoon peanut oil
4 shallot segments (about 2 tablespoons), sliced

Sambal Chilli
6 medium dried red chillies, seeds removed and soaked in hot water, to soften
1 garlic clove, peeled and roughly chopped
Large pinch of salt
2 candle nuts

Garnish
Crispy fried shallots (available from Asian food stores)

Serves 2

Method

Sambal Chilli
Drain the chillies and grind to a paste with the garlic, salt and candle nuts.

Spicy Shrimp Broth
To make the stock, place the shrimp heads and shells in a pot with the water and salt and bring to the boil. When just boiling, add the shrimp, reduce the heat and simmer for 4 minutes. Remove the shrimp and set aside for later use.

Bring the chicken stock to the boil in a large pan and reduce to a simmer.

Strain the shrimp stock into the chicken stock and continue to simmer.

Heat a wok over medium heat and add the oil. Add the shallots and fry until browned and crisp.

Add the Sambal Chilli and fry for about 3 minutes, or until aromatic, stirring constantly.

Add the contents of the wok to the stock with a pinch of salt. At this stage, either continue to simmer while finishing the recipe or turn off the heat and store until ready to reheat and serve.

To Serve
Bring a large pan of water to the boil. Cook the noodles, beansprouts and kangkung for about 30 seconds.

Drain and divide between 2 large soup bowls. Top with half the boiled egg, fish cake, pork and shrimp. Fill the bowls with broth. Garnish with crispy fried shallots.

> **Alternatives & Variations**
> • Sliced fish balls (2 or 3 to each serve) can be used instead of fish cake.
> • Use a commercial chilli paste (sambal oelek) instead of the Sambal Chilli.

Nonya Laksa [Spicy Coconut Soup with Noodles and Fish Balls]

Nonya Laksa is perhaps the best known Nonya soup. It has a spicy coconut milk soup base to which noodles and a selection of seafood, meat and/or vegetables are added. It is very versatile and there are hundreds of different versions. It is not to be confused with Penang's laksa assam, which is a tamarind-based broth.

Ingredients

8 slices fish cake
8 small fish balls
1 cup (4¾ oz/140 g) loosely packed thin fresh egg noodles (
1 cup (4¾ oz/140 g) loosely packed thin rice noodles (vermicelli), soaked in hot water for 15 minutes and drained
¾–1¼ in (2–3 cm) piece cucumber, julienned
2 teaspoons spring onions (scallions), chopped
1 hard-boiled egg, halved
3 cups (1¼ pints/750 ml) Laksa Gravy

LAKSA GRAVY
3 tablespoons peanut oil
4 tablespoons Spice Paste (see below)
1½ cups (12 fl oz/375 ml) coconut milk
2½ cups (18 fl oz/550 ml) Chicken Stock
½ teaspoon salt, or to taste
¼ teaspoon sugar, or to taste

SPICE PASTE (MAKES 4 TABLESPOONS)
1 stalk lemongrass, roughly sliced
10 medium long red dried chillies, soaked in hot water for 20 minutes and drained
4 garlic cloves
¾ in (2 cm) piece turmeric, chopped
½ tablespoon galangal, roughly chopped
3 tablespoons shallots, roughly chopped
2 teaspoons ground coriander
¼ teaspoon dried shrimp, crushed
3 candle nuts

TO SERVE
Fresh beansprouts
SERVES 2

Method

SPICE PASTE
Place all ingredients in a food processor and chop finely. Transfer to a mortar and pound until smooth and evenly coloured.

LAKSA GRAVY
Place the oil in a large pan over medium-low heat, add the spice paste and fry for about 5 minutes, stirring constantly until fragrant and the oil starts to separate.

Add the coconut milk and stock. Bring to the boil then reduce heat to low and simmer for 5 minutes. Stir in the salt and sugar.

TO SERVE
Heat the fish balls and fish cake in the simmering Laksa Gravy for a few minutes.

Cook the noodles in boiling water for 30 seconds or until soft. Drain and place in soup bowls.

Top the noodles with half of the cucumber, spring onion, fish cake slices, fish balls, beancurd, cockles and hard-boiled egg. Fill the bowls with Laksa Gravy and serve.

Alternatives & Variations
• Use 3 macadamia nuts or 6 blanched almonds instead of candle nuts.
• Use ½ teaspoon ground turmeric instead of fresh.
• Use ginger instead of galangal. The flavour will be slightly different but still delicious.
• Laksa can be made with any type of seafood or with chicken. If raw, place in the laksa gravy and simmer until cooked.
• Serve with some fresh beansprouts.

Singapore Chilli Crab

The luxurious dish had a tomato and chilli-based sauce. It's so popular that it is the signature dish of Singapore.

Ingredients

1 raw mud crab, weighing about 2¼ lb (1 kg)
1 tablespoon Fried Chilli Paste (Sambal Goreng Lombok, *see* recipe)
2 tablespoons tomato sauce
2 tablespoons chilli sauce
1 tablespoon oyster sauce
2 teaspoons sugar
½ teaspoon salt
1 tablespoon vegetable oil
1 tablespoon garlic, minced (crushed)
1 cup (8 fl oz/250 ml) chicken or pork stock
1 egg white

GARNISH
Coriander (cilantro) leaves

SERVES 2

Method

To prepare the crab; remove the large claws, remove and discard the flap from the body section. Pull the body away from the back shell and remove and discard the gills and stomach sac. Cut the body section into 4 pieces and crack the large claw shells with the back of a heavy knife. Wash the crab and drain. Scrub the back shell and keep it whole to use as a garnish.

Combine the Fried Chilli Paste, tomato sauce and chilli sauce in a small bowl. Combine the oyster sauce, sugar and salt in another.

Heat a wok over medium-high heat and add the oil. Fry the garlic for 10 seconds, stirring constantly.

Add the Fried Chilli Paste, tomato and chilli sauces and cook for another 10 seconds, stirring. Add the stock, oyster sauce, sugar and salt and stir again.

Increase the heat to high and bring to a fast boil. Add the crab pieces (including the back shell), stir to settle it into the liquid and cook for 3 minutes, stirring occasionally and turning the larger pieces once. Remove the back shell.

Drizzle in the egg white and stir gently until there are white streaks through the sauce.

Place on a serving dish, arrange the back shell on top and garnish with coriander leaves. Serve with Chinese steamed or baked buns, rice or bread and a finger bowl.

Alternatives & Variations
• Use 3 blue swimmer or any medium crabs. Remove the large claws and cut the bodies in half.
• Use a commercial chilli paste (sambal oelek).

Prawn and Pineapple Curry

This is a smooth, sweet and fairly mild curry and is equally delicious when made with chicken.

Ingredients

1 tablespoon peanut oil
1 cup (8 fl oz/250 ml) coconut milk
1½ cups (9 oz/250 g)pineapple pieces, fresh or canned
12 large shrimp, shelled and deveined
1 cup (8 fl oz/250 ml) coconut cream
Salt and pepper, to taste
1 quantity Curry Paste (*see* below)

Curry Paste

4 large red dried chillies, seeded and soaked in hot water for 15 minutes
4 fresh red chillies, seeded and roughly chopped
8 shallot segments (about 4½ tablespoons), roughly chopped
1 stalk lemongrass, finely chopped
1¼ in (3 cm) piece fresh ginger, roughly chopped
1 teaspoon ground turmeric
4 candle nuts

To Serve

Plain rice

Serves 3–4

Method

Curry Paste

Drain the dried chillies and grind with the fresh chillies, shallots, lemongrass, ginger, turmeric and candle nuts in a mortar or in a small food processor until a fairly smooth paste.

Curry

Heat a wok over low heat and add the oil. Add the Curry Paste, increase the heat to medium and fry for 3–5 minutes, stirring constantly until the oil starts to separate.

Add the coconut milk and pineapple pieces, bring to the boil then reduce the heat to low and simmer for 3 minutes.

Add the shrimp, coconut cream, salt and pepper and continue to cook over low heat for about 5 minutes or until the shrimp are cooked.

Serve with plain rice.

Alternatives & Variations
- This dish can also be made with chicken. Use chicken on the bone cut into 1¾–2 in (4–5 cm) pieces. Add the thin coconut milk, simmer for 10 minutes. Then add coconut cream, pineapple pieces and seasoning and simmer for another 10 minutes.
- Use 4 macadamia nuts or 8 blanched almonds instead of candle nuts.

Sambal Goreng Sotong [Squid Sambal]

Squid sambal is deliciously rich and spicy making it best served as part of a shared meal.

Ingredients

5 medium squid
1 quantity Spice Paste (*see* below)
1 tablespoon peanut oil
1–2 stalks lemongrass, thinly sliced
  (about 1 tablespoon)
¼ cup (2 fl oz/60 ml) tamarind liquid
  (soak 2 teaspoons tamarind pulp in ¼
  cup (2 fl oz/60 ml) hot water and strain
  when cool)
2 teaspoons palm sugar, grated
  (shredded)
Salt, to taste

Spice Paste
5 large red dried chillies, seeded and
  toasted in a dry pan until crisp
5 candle nuts
4 shallot segments (about 2 tablespoons),
  roughly chopped
¼ teaspoon shrimp paste, toasted over a
  gas flame or wrapped in foil and lightly
  toasted over an electric element

Serves 4 as part of a shared meal

Method

Preparing the Squid
If using whole, uncleaned squid clean them by slitting the tube open and slicing through the head to flatten the whole squid. Scrape out the innards. Remove the head and tentacles and remove the small round 'beak' that is in the centre of the tentacles. Remove the quill from the tube. Wash thoroughly in three changes of water and dry on paper towels.

Cut each tube in half and score the flattened tubes on the inside horizontally and vertically then slice into strips about 1¼ in (3 cm) wide.

Cut the tentacles into ¾–1¼ in (2–3 cm) lengths and the head section into quarters.

Spice Paste
Grind the chillies and candle nuts to a powder in a mortar or small food processor.

Add the shallots and shrimp paste and continue to grind to a paste.

Cooking the Squid
Heat a wok over medium-low heat and add the oil. Add the spice paste and lemongrass and fry, stirring constantly for 3–5 minutes until the oil starts to separate.

Stir in the tamarind liquid and palm sugar.

Add the prepared squid and stir. Reduce the heat to low and cook uncovered, stirring frequently for about 6 minutes until the squid is cooked. Add salt to taste.

Alternatives & Variations
• Use brown sugar instead of palm sugar.
• Use 5 macadamia nuts or 10 blanched almonds instead of candle nuts. Use
  4 macadamia nuts or 8 blanched almonds instead of candle nuts.

Hainan Steamed Chicken Rice

This dish consists of succulent steamed chicken with two sauces, soy and chilli, fluffy rice cooked in chicken broth and flavoursome chicken soup to pour over or serve separately. This recipe may look complicated but it is actually quite simple and very enjoyable to make. It can be made ahead of time (the rice will stay hot for an hour or more). The chicken can be served cold, or can be reheated by pouring a cup of piping hot soup over it, then draining.

Ingredients

STEAMED CHICKEN
8 cups (3½ pints/2 litres) Chicken Stock or water (enough to cover chicken)
3 cm (1¼ in) piece fresh ginger, lightly bruised
2 large garlic cloves, peeled and lightly bruised
1 teaspoon peanut oil
1 teaspoon salt
1 chicken, weighing 2¼–3½ lb (1–1.5 kg)

SOY SAUCE MIX
½ cup (4 fl oz/125 ml) light soy sauce
1 spring onion (scallion), halved
1 teaspoon thick black soy sauce (also sold as caramel sauce)

CHILLI SAUCE
3 long red chillies, seeded and roughly chopped
1 garlic clove, peeled and roughly chopped
½ oz (15 g) fresh root ginger, roughly chopped
1 tablespoon cold water
¼ teaspoon salt, or to taste
¼ teaspoon garlic (extra), minced
1–2 tablespoons hot water

Method

STEAMED CHICKEN
Tie a piece of string around the middle of the chicken and make a loop about 4 in (10 cm) long to make it easier to remove from the pan.

Place the water, ginger, garlic, oil and salt in a pan that will comfortably hold the chicken. When simmering but not boiling, gently lower the chicken in. If necessary, add extra hot water to cover the chicken.

Cook very gently for 35 minutes (for a 2¼ lb/1 kg chicken) or 40 minutes (for a 3½ lb /1.5 kg chicken). Do not boil; you just need to keep the water hot.

Lift the chicken out using the string and place in a basin of salted cold water for 15 minutes. Strain the chicken stock resulting from this process and set aside.

SOY SAUCE MIX
Heat the light soy sauce and spring onion until hot. Stir in the black soy sauce and allow to cool.

Discard the spring onion before serving.

CHILLI SAUCE
Place the chillies, garlic, ginger and cold water in a blender and blend until smooth. Transfer to a small bowl and add the extra minced garlic, salt and hot water.

Stir and allow to cool before serving.

Alternatives & Variations
• Pandan leaves can be omitted if not available.
• To make a quicker version of soy sauce, mix together light soy sauce, a few drops of sesame oil and a little honey.
• To make a quick chilli sauce mix the fried garlic and ginger from the cooking of the rice with bottled sweet chilli sauce.

RICE

2 teaspoons peanut oil

1 teaspoon garlic, minced

1½ teaspoons fresh ginger, minced

2 cups (14 oz/400 g)long-grain rice, rinsed and well drained

3½ cups (1½ pints/875 ml) Chicken Stock (reserved from steaming the chicken)

½ teaspoon salt

1 pandan leaf, cut into thirds

SOUP

4 cups (1¾ pints/1 litre) Chicken Stock (reserved from steaming the chicken)

1 garlic clove, peeled and lightly bruised

Salt, to taste

1 teaspoon sugar, or to taste

1 pandan leaf, tied in a knot

1 cup (4 oz/115 g) mixed white cabbage and Asian greens, roughly chopped and steamed

GARNISHES

1 medium cucumber, cut in half lengthways and sliced

1 teaspoon peanut oil

2 spring onions (scallions), chopped

½ cup (1¾ oz/50 g) fresh beansprouts

SERVES 4

RICE

Heat the oil in a large pan over medium heat and fry the garlic and ginger until golden. Remove and discard (or set aside if you wish to make the quick chilli sauce below).

Add the rice to the flavoured oil and stir until coated. Add the chicken stock and salt, and bring to the boil, stirring once or twice.

Arrange the pandan leaf pieces on top, turn the heat as low as possible, cover and cook for 20 minutes.

Remove from the heat and leave for 10 minutes or longer. Fluff up the rice with a fork before serving.

SOUP

Place the chicken stock in a pan, add the bruised garlic clove, salt to taste, sugar and pandan leaf and heat until simmering.

When ready to serve, divide the cabbage and greens between 4 soup bowls and fill up with soup.

TO SERVE

Cut the chicken in half using a cleaver or very sharp knife. Remove the wing, leg and thigh. Remove the breast from the bone and cut into ¾ in (2 cm) slices. Remove the meat from the thigh bone and slice. (You can set the wings and drumsticks aside to use as snacks.)

Place the sliced chicken on a bed of sliced cucumber. Pour 1 tablespoon of the Soy Sauce Mix and ¼ teaspoon of oil over the chicken. Garnish with the spring onion and fresh beansprouts.

Serve one plate of rice and one bowl of chicken soup to each person separately. Place the chilli sauce and remaining Soy Sauce Mix on the table as condiments.

Ayam Pong Teh [Chicken with Soybean Paste, Potatoes and Mushrooms]

This is a delicious, quick and easy dish of Nonya origin. Nonya cuisine (also referred to as Peranakan or Straits Chinese cuisine) developed as a result of Malay women marrying Chinese men and cooking Chinese-style dishes using Malay ingredients.

Ingredients

2 tablespoons vegetable oil
4 tablespoons shallots, puréed
2 tablespoons garlic, puréed
1½ tablespoons soybean paste
1 lb 2 oz (500 g) chicken, cut into 1¾ in (4 cm) pieces, on the bone
1½–2 cups (12–16 fl oz/350–475 ml) water
2 medium potatoes, peeled and cut into wedges
5–6 button (white) mushrooms, halved
1 teaspoon sweet soy sauce (kecap manis)
3 teaspoons sugar

TO SERVE
Plain rice

SERVES 2 OR 3

Method

Heat a wok over medium-high heat and add the oil. Fry the shallots and garlic for 2–3 minutes, stirring constantly until dry and lightly browned.

Add the soybean paste and continue frying for 2–3 minutes, stirring constantly. Add the chicken and stir to coat with the paste, gradually add the 1½ cups of water and then the potatoes.

Bring to the boil and cook for 3 minutes over medium-high heat, then stir in the mushrooms, kecap manis and sugar.

Lower the heat to medium-low and continue cooking for about 15–20 minutes, stirring occasionally, until the chicken and potatoes are cooked. Serve with plain rice.

Alternatives & Variations
• Brown or white onion can be used instead of shallots.
• This dish can also be made with pork or pork ribs (see recipe).

Char Siew [Chinese Sweet Roast Pork]

Char Siew (also called barbecue pork) is a versatile Asian treat. It is used in a multitude of other dishes from stir-fries to soups or is equally delicious served sliced on a bed of cucumber with plain rice and a small bowl each of chilli sauce and light soy sauce.

Ingredients

¾ cup (5 oz/150 g) white (granulated)
   sugar
¼ teaspoon white pepper
½ teaspoon five spice powder
1 lb 2 oz–1 lb 11 oz (500–750 g) pork
   fillet, cut into strips about ¾–1¼ in
   (2–3 cm) square and about 8 in
   (20 cm) long
2 teaspoons thick black soy sauce (also
   sold as caramel sauce)
2 teaspoons light soy sauce
2 teaspoons Chinese cooking wine or
   dry sherry
1–2 small pinches red food colouring
   powder (optional)

To Serve
1 medium cucumber, peeled and chopped
   into chunks
Plain rice
Chilli sauce
Light soy sauce with sliced fresh red chilli

Serves 4–6

Method

MARINATING
In a large bowl, mix together the sugar, pepper, five spice powder, sauces, cooking wine and colouring until well combined.

Add the pork strips and rub the marinade well into the meat. Cover and refrigerate overnight, or for at least 7 hours.

BARBECUING THE PORK
Preheat the oven to 240°C/475°C/Gas mark 9

Pour ¼ in (0.5 cm) of boiling water into a flat-base roasting pan and place a wire rack over the top of the pan.

Mix the pork again and arrange the strips quite close together on the wire rack. Pour over any remaining marinade. Roast for 15–20 minutes until the edges are caramelised and the pork is cooked.

PORK GRAVY
If you want gravy to use in other Asian noodle and soup dishes, stir and reduce the pan juices over high heat to a thick syrupy gravy.

TO SERVE
Serve the pork thinly sliced, on a bed of chunky chopped cucumber, with plain rice, chilli sauce and light soy sauce with chilli on the side.

Alternatively use in soups, stir-fries, fried rice, salads or Chinese baked or steamed buns.

Alternatives & Variations
• Pork fillet (preferably with some fat) or even pork belly strips (skin and bones removed) can be used instead of scotch fillet.
• Sweet soy sauce (kecap manis) could be substituted for caramel sauce.

Ayam Buah Keras [Candle Nut Chicken]

This is a deliciously aromatic and spicy dish of Nonya origin.

Ingredients

1 lb 2 oz (500 g) chicken pieces (on
the bone), cut into about 2 in (5 cm)
pieces
¼ teaspoon salt
2 teaspoons sugar
1¼ cups (½ pint/300 ml) water or more
4 kaffir lime leaves
4 turmeric leaves (if available)

CANDLE NUT SPICE PASTE
½ teaspoon shrimp paste
3 teaspoons chilli powder
½ teaspoon ground turmeric
5 shallot segments (about 3 tablespoons),
chopped
1 tablespoon fresh ginger, roughly
chopped
3 garlic cloves, peeled and roughly
chopped
1 stalk lemongrass (about 1 tablespoon),
chopped
½ teaspoon salt
1 teaspoon palm sugar
10 candle nuts
2 kaffir lime leaves
1 turmeric leaf
2 tablespoons peanut oil

TO SERVE
Plain rice

SERVES 2

Method

CANDLE NUT SPICE PASTE
Toast the shrimp paste over a gas flame or wrap in foil and toast over a low electric element for 1–2 minutes, turning a few times until browned and slightly crisp.

Place all the spice paste ingredients except the candle nuts, leaves and oil in a mortar or food processor and grind to a thick paste. Add the candle nuts and continue to grind until you have a fairly smooth paste.

Heat a wok over medium heat and add the oil. Add the spice paste and leaves and fry for 1–2 minutes until the oil is absorbed.

Now lower the heat to medium-low and continue to fry for 4–5 minutes, or until the oil starts to separate again. Stir frequently to prevent burning. Discard the leaves. At this stage, either store the spice paste for later use, or continue with the recipe.

CHICKEN
Add the chicken to the fried spice paste and stir-fry over medium heat for 4 minutes. Add the salt and sugar and stir.

Add 1 cup (8 fl oz/250 ml) of the water and the kaffir lime and turmeric leaves. Bring to the boil, reduce the heat to medium-low and cook for 10 minutes, stirring occasionally.

Add the remaining water (or more for a thinner sauce) and cook for another 5 minutes, or until the chicken is cooked. Serve with plain rice.

Alternatives & Variations
• 1 small brown or white onion can be used instead of shallots.
• Substitute 6 raw macadamia nuts or 18 blanched raw almonds for candle nuts.
• Turmeric leaves can be omitted without making too much difference.
• This dish can also be made with beef, fish balls or fresh fish.

Hainan Roasted Chicken Rice

Even though this is called roasted chicken, the poultry here is actually deep-fried after having been stuffed with five spice powder and rubbed with a honey soy mixture. This recipe is best attempted if you have a very large wok or deep fat fryer as the chicken should float in the bubbling oil. An alternative is to deep-fry it in a wok for part of the cooking time and finish it off in the oven. Due to its high fat content, while sensational in flavour, this is not a dish you would want to cook every day, but it is well worth the effort for a special treat.

Ingredients

Vegetable oil, for deep-frying
1 tablespoon dark soy sauce
½ tablespoon honey
1 teaspoon five spice powder
1 chicken, weighing 2¼–3½ lb (1–1.5kg)

Soy Sauce
½ cup (4 fl oz/125 g) light soy sauce
1 spring onion, cut in half
1 teaspoon thick black soy sauce (also
    sold as caramel sauce)

Chilli Sauce
3 long red chillies (1¾ oz/50 g), seeded
    and roughly chopped
1 garlic clove, peeled and roughly
    chopped
1½ tablespoons (½ oz/15 g) fresh ginger,
    roughly chopped
1 tablespoon cold water
¼ teaspoon garlic (extra), minced
¼ teaspoon salt
1–2 tablespoons hot water

Rice
2 teaspoons peanut oil
1 teaspoon garlic, minced (crushed)
1½ teaspoons ginger, minced (crushed)
2 cups (14 oz./400 g) long-grain rice,
    rinsed and well drained
3½ cups (1½ pints/875 ml) chicken stock
    (see recipe)
½ teaspoon salt
1 pandan leaf, cut into thirds

Method

Pour the oil into a large wok and heat until very hot.

Meanwhile, mix together the soy sauce and honey. Rub the five spice powder around the cavity of the chicken. Rub the honey soy mix all over the outside of the bird.

Carefully lower the chicken into the hot oil. Fry for 15 minutes, turn over and fry for another 15 minutes.

Carefully remove with tongs and drain over a plate. Deep-fry it, in as much oil as will safely fit in the wok, for 4 minutes on each side, then move the chicken to a roasting pan and roast in a moderate oven for 30 minutes (40 minutes for the larger chicken).

Soy Sauce Mix
Heat the light soy sauce and spring onion until hot.

Stir in the black soy sauce, allow to cool and discard the spring onion before serving.

Chilli Sauce
Place the chillies, garlic, ginger and cold water in a blender and blend until smooth.

Transfer to a small bowl and add the extra minced garlic, salt and hot water. Stir and allow to cool before serving.

Rice
Heat the oil in a large pan over medium heat and fry the garlic and ginger until golden. Remove and discard (or set aside if you wish to make the quick chilli sauce below).

Add the rice to the flavoured oil and stir until coated. Add the chicken stock and salt and bring to the boil stirring once or twice.

Arrange the pandan leaf pieces on top, turn the heat as low as possible, cover and cook for 20 minutes.

Remove from the heat and leave for 10 minutes or longer. Fluff the rice up with a fork before serving.

SOUP

4 cups (1¾ pints/1 litre) chicken stock
   (*see* recipe)
1 garlic clove, peeled and lightly bruised
Salt, to taste
½ teaspoon sugar
1 pandan leaf, tied in knot
1 cup (4 oz/115 g) mixed white cabbage
   and Asian greens, roughly chopped and
   steamed

GARNISHES

1 medium cucumber, cut in half
   lengthways and sliced
1 teaspoon peanut oil
2 spring onions (scallions), chopped
½ cup (1¾ oz/50 g) fresh beansprouts

SERVES 4

SOUP

Pour the chicken stock into a pan, add the garlic, salt, sugar and pandan leaf and heat until simmering.

Divide the cabbage and greens between the soup bowls and fill with soup.

TO SERVE

Cut the chicken in half. Remove the wing, leg and thigh. Remove the breast from the bone and cut into ¾ in (2 cm) slices. Remove the meat from the thighbone and slice. (You can set the wings and drumsticks aside to use as snacks.)

Place the sliced chicken on a bed of sliced cucumber. Pour 1 tablespoon of the Soy Sauce Mix and ¼ teaspoon of oil over the chicken.

Garnish with spring onion and fresh beansprouts.

Serve one plate of rice and one bowl of chicken soup to each person separately. Place the chilli sauce and remaining Soy Sauce Mix on the table as condiments.

> **Alternatives & Variations**
> - Pandan leaves can be omitted if not available.
> - To make a quicker version of soy sauce, mix together light soy sauce, a few drops of sesame oil and a little honey.
> - To make a quick chilli sauce mix the fried garlic and ginger (from the cooking of the rice) with bottled sweet chilli sauce.

Tandoori Chicken

This recipe is extremely delicious and differs from traditional tandoori chicken in that yogurt is not used in the marinade. Excellent accompaniments for this dish are Dahl, Mint Chutney and Mushtaq's Naan or Garlic Naan.

Ingredients

1 cup (8 fl oz/250 ml) Chilli Boh (*see* below)
½ cup (4 fl oz/125 ml) tamarind liquid (soak 1 tablespoon tamarind pulp in ½ cup (4 fl oz/125 ml)warm water, stir well and drain off the liquid when cool)
1 teaspoon salt
1 tablespoon Indian meat curry powder
2 fl oz (60 ml) vegetable or canola oil
1¾ lb (1 kg) chicken pieces, skinned

CHILLI BOH
8 large mild dried red chillies, stems, seeds and membranes removed and roughly chopped
1 cup (8 fl oz/250 ml) boiling water
1 large garlic clove
¼ teaspoon salt

SERVES 4

Method

CHILLI BOH
Soak the chillies in boiling water for about 30 minutes until softened.

Place the chillies, liquid, garlic and salt in an electric blender. Blend until you have a smooth sauce.

TANDOORI CHICKEN
Mix together the tamarind liquid and salt. Add the curry powder, Chilli Boh and oil, mixing after each addition.

Place the chicken pieces in a large bowl and pour the marinade over. Mix well, cover and set aside for at least 15 minutes (or overnight). Refrigerate if marinating for a long time.

Preheat the oven to 180°C/350°F/Gas mark 4.

Remove the chicken from the marinade and place on a rack in a baking dish.

Roast for 30 minutes then increase the heat to 220°C/425°F/Gas mark 7 and roast for another 20 minutes, or until the chicken is nicely coloured and the juices run clear. The chicken can also be barbecued or cooked in a tandoori oven.

Alternatives & Variations
• Instead of making tamarind liquid, mix 1 tablespoon of tamarind concentrate with the ½ cup (4 fl oz/125 ml) of water.
• Use a curry powder where the main ingredients are coriander, aniseed, cumin, cinnamon, cardamom, pepper, star anise and cloves or the nearest equivalent available.
• Use a mild, unsweetened chilli sauce instead of making Chilli Boh.

Devil Chicken Curry

Devil (or Debal in Malay) chicken curry is a Eurasian dish that is said to have originated in Malacca. The use of vinegar and English mustard adds a nice tang to the dish.

Ingredients

8 large chicken drumsticks
3 tablespoons peanut oil
1 teaspoon salt
6 shallot segments, sliced
3 garlic cloves, peeled and thinly sliced
1 tablespoon black mustard seeds
1½ –2 cups (12–16 fl oz/350–475 ml)
    water
1½ tablespoons white vinegar
½ tablespoon dark soy sauce
½ tablespoon prepared English mustard
Salt, to taste

Curry Paste
25 large red dried chillies, seeded and
    soaked in hot water for about
    10 minutes, to soften
6 fresh red chillies, seeded and roughly
    chopped
1 cup (4 oz/115 g) shallot segments,
    roughly chopped
3 garlic cloves
2 teaspoons ginger, roughly chopped
8 candle nuts
1 tablespoon ground turmeric
1 tablespoon ground coriander

To Serve
Plain rice

Serves 4

Method

Curry Paste
Drain the dried chillies and place in a mortar or food processor with all of the remaining spice paste ingredients. Pound or process until you have a fairly smooth, evenly coloured paste.

Chicken
Dust the drumsticks with salt and set aside.

Heat the oil in a large pan set over medium heat, add the sliced shallots and garlic and fry for about 2 minutes, or until the shallots are starting to brown. Add the Curry Paste and mustard seeds and continue to fry, stirring almost constantly for about 5 minutes until aromatic and starting to look a bit oily.

Add the drumsticks, stir well to coat with the curry paste and fry until they start to change colour.

Add the water, bring to the boil then reduce the heat to low and simmer for 1 hour, or until the chicken is tender.

Stir in the vinegar, dark soy sauce, English mustard and salt to taste. Serve with plain rice.

Bak Siou [Nonya Pork Ribs]

This is a deliciously different way to cook pork spare ribs.

Ingredients

1 tablespoon vegetable oil
1 lb 13 oz (750 g) pork spare ribs, cut
   into 2 in (5 cm) pieces
2 cups (16 fl oz/500 ml) water

CORIANDER AND VINEGAR PASTE
2 tablespoons tamarind liquid made from
   tamarind pulp
2 tablespoons ground coriander
¼ cup (2 fl oz/60 ml) white vinegar
¼ cup (1 oz/30 g) shallot segments,
   roughly chopped
1 tablespoon palm sugar
¼ teaspoon salt

TO SERVE
Plain rice

SERVES 3 OR 4

Method

CORIANDER AND VINEGAR PASTE
Soak half the tamarind pulp in 2½ tablespoons hot water. Stir and strain when cool.

Toast the coriander in a dry wok or pan over low heat until aromatic.

Place all of the paste ingredients in a blender and blend until smooth.

PORK RIBS
Heat a wok or large pan over medium-low heat and add the oil. Fry the paste for 4 minutes, stirring frequently. Add the ribs and stir well to coat with paste.

Add the water, bring to the boil, reduce the heat, cover and simmer for 1 hour. Uncover and simmer for another 30 minutes until the pork is tender, stirring occasionally. Serve with plain rice.

Alternatives & Variations
• Onion can be used instead of shallots.
• Brown or white sugar can be substituted for palm sugar.
• This dish freezes well so make a larger quantity and freeze for up to 3 months. When required, defrost, then reheat in a wok adding enough water to achieve the desired consistency.
• This dish can also be made with mutton, beef or duck.

Babi Pong Teh [Pork with Soybean Paste, Potatoes and Mushrooms]

Ingredients

2 tablespoons vegetable oil

4 tablespoons very finely minced or
   puréed shallots

2 tablespoons very finely minced or
   puréed garlic

1½ tablespoons soybean paste

1 lb 2 oz (500 g) pork ribs, cut into
   2–2¼ in (5–6 cm) pieces

2–2½ cups (16–18 fl oz/475–550 ml)
   water

2 medium potatoes, peeled and cut into
   wedges

5–6 button (white) mushrooms, halved

1 teaspoon sweet soy sauce (kecap manis)

3 teaspoons sugar

TO SERVE
Plain rice

SERVES 2

Method

Heat a wok over medium-high heat and add the oil.

Fry the shallots and garlic for 2–3 minutes, stirring constantly until dry and lightly browned. Add the soybean paste and continue frying for 2–3 minutes, stirring constantly.

Add the pork and stir to coat with paste, gradually add 2 cups (16 fl oz/500 ml) of water. Bring to the boil then reduce the heat to low, cover and simmer for about 30–40 minutes, or until the meat is almost tender.

Add the potatoes, mushrooms, kecap manis and sugar and continue to simmer, uncovered for about 15–20 minutes, stirring occasionally, until the potatoes are cooked. Add an extra ½ cup (8 fl oz/250 ml) of water during this time if you prefer a thinner sauce. Serve with plain rice.

> **Alternatives & Variations**
> • Brown or white onion can be used instead of shallots.
> • This dish can also be made with chicken (*see* Ayam Pong Teh recipe).

Beehoon Goreng [Stir-Fried Vermicelli Noodles with Pork and Fish Balls]

This is a very simple fried noodle dish. It is a great way to use up a small amount of leftover Char Siew (barbecue pork, see recipe).

Ingredients

2 teaspoons vegetable oil
2 tablespoons raw pork, thinly sliced
3 large or 6 small fish balls, halved
8 thin slices fish cake (available from some Asian food stores)
1 cup (4 oz/115 g) Asian greens, cut into ¾ in (2 cm) slices
½ cup (8 fl oz/250 ml) chicken or pork stock (see recipes)
2 teaspoons thick black soy sauce (also sold as caramel sauce in Asian food stores)
3½ oz (100 g) vermicelli noodles, soaked in hot water for 15 minutes and well drained
2 teaspoons Crispy Fried Garlic (see recipe)
10 thin slices barbecue pork (see recipe)

Sauce

2 tablespoons light soy sauce
1–2 small green chillies, sliced

Serves 2

Method

Sauce

Combine the light soy sauce and sliced chilli. Place in a small sauce dish and set aside.

Noodles

Heat a wok over high heat and add the oil. Toss in the raw pork, fish balls, fish cake and greens. Stir quickly until the pork has changed colour then add ¼ cup (2 oz/60 ml) of the stock and 1 teaspoon of the soy sauce.

Cover the wok for 10 seconds then uncover and push these ingredients to one side (the liquid needs to evaporate). If your wok is small, set aside these ingredients on a plate.

Add the noodles and remaining stock to the wok. Stir briefly (keeping the noodles separate from the other ingredients) and cover the wok again for 10 seconds. Uncover, add the remaining soy sauce and the Crispy Garlic.

Stir-fry the noodles (still keeping them separate from the other ingredients) until coated with the sauce for 1 minute, or until the liquid is mostly absorbed. Divide the noodles between two plates.

Briefly stir-fry the pork, fish balls etc. again and place on top of the noodles along with the barbecue pork slices. Serve the sauce alongside as a condiment.

> Alternatives & Variations
> • Use extra fish balls (2 or 3 to each serve) instead of fish cake.

Char Koay Teow [Malaysian Fried Noodles]

This Chinese-inspired fried noodle dish, which can be found all over Malaysia, uses wide flat rice noodles. Traditionally Char Koay Teow contains clams but it is equally delicious without them if they are difficult to obtain or out of season.

Ingredients

1 teaspoon chilli paste (sambal oelek)
2 teaspoons thick black soy sauce (also sold as caramel sauce)
2 teaspoons light soy sauce
2 teaspoons oyster sauce
5 oz (150 g) thick flat rice noodles, covered with boiling water, soaked for 15 minutes and drained
1 tablespoon vegetable oil
6 raw peeled large shrimp (prawns)
8 strips raw squid
1 tablespoon garlic, minced
2 eggs
1 large handful beansprouts
1 tablespoon clam meat
2 tablespoons water

SERVES 2

Method

For speed and convenience, combine the chilli paste and sauces in a small bowl.

Heat a wok over medium-high heat and add the oil. Add the shrimp and squid and stir-fry for about 10 seconds. Add the garlic and fry for another 10 seconds, stirring constantly.

Crack in the eggs and stir gently until just cooked. Add the noodles and stir briefly. Add the combined sauces.

Increase the heat to high and stir-fry until the noodles are coated with sauce. Add the beansprouts and clams and stir through.

Splash the water in around the sides of the wok and stir-fry for about 15 seconds or until well combined but not too dry. Serve immediately.

Alternatives & Variations
• Use sweet soy sauce (kecap manis) instead of thick black soy sauce.
• This dish can also be made with sliced pork or chicken. Stir-fry until cooked before adding the garlic.

Nasi Lemak

[Coconut Rice with Spicy Chicken Curry, Crispy Anchovies, Peanuts and Boiled Egg]

Nasi Lemak literally means 'coconut rice'. In Malaysia and Singapore, it is always served with a very spicy chilli sambal. The recipe is my version of Nasi Lemak, where the sauce from the curry doubles as a chilli sambal.

Ingredients

½ quantity Devil Chicken Curry (*see* recipe)
½ quantity Sambal Ikan Teri (*see* recipe)
12 cucumber slices
4 hard-boiled eggs, quartered

COCONUT RICE
2 cups (14 oz/200 g) long-grain or basmati rice
½ teaspoon salt
1 cup (8 fl oz/250 ml) coconut milk
1 cup (8 fl oz/250 ml) water

SERVES 4

Method

COCONUT RICE
Wash the rice and drain well. Place in a pan with the salt, coconut cream and water. Bring to the boil, stirring to prevent the rice from sticking.

Reduce the heat to very low, cover with a tight lid and cook for 15 minutes.

Remove from the heat and leave to stand for another 10 minutes before lifting the lid. Fluff the rice with a fork before serving.

TO SERVE
Place a mound of rice in the middle of a plate.

Surround with a piece of chicken from the curry, a pile of Sambal Ikan Teri, some cucumber slices and the quartered hard-boiled egg.

Fried Hokkien Mee [Singapore Fried Noodles]

Fried Hokkien Mee is a typical Singaporean noodle dish and you will find a stall selling it at every food centre in Singapore. It is quick and easy to make and is an ideal lunch dish.

Ingredients

7 oz (200 g) fresh Hokkien egg noodles, prepared according to packet instructions

1¾ oz (50 g) rice vermicelli noodles, covered with boiling water, soaked for 15 minutes and drained well

5 teaspoons peanut or vegetable oil

1 egg, lightly beaten

1 tablespoon garlic, peeled and finely chopped

¾ cup (6 fl oz/175 ml) chicken or pork stock (see recipes)

1 tablespoon garlic chives, cut into 1¼ in (3 cm) lengths

½ teaspoon thick black soy sauce (also sold as caramel sauce)

¼ teaspoon salt

10 cooked and peeled shrimp (prawns) (see note below)

½ cup (2¼ oz/70 g) cooked squid (see note)

Garnishes

2 teaspoons Fried Chilli Paste (Sambal Goreng Lombok, see recipe)

½ small lime, halved

1 tablespoon pork crackling, roughly chopped (optional)

1 red chilli, sliced

Serves 2

Method

Mix together both types of noodles.

Heat a wok over medium heat and add 2 teaspoons of the oil. Pour in the egg and tilt the wok toward you. Keep pushing the egg to the back of the wok with a spatula until it is just cooked. Remove to a plate and roughly chop it.

Heat the remaining 3 teaspoons of oil, add the garlic and fry for about 20 seconds, stirring constantly.

Increase the heat to high and add the chopped omelette, stock, noodles, garlic chives, soy sauce and salt. Stir, cover the wok and cook for 45 seconds. Remove the lid and stir until the liquid has evaporated and been absorbed into the noodles. Add the shrimp and squid. Stir through and turn off the heat.

Serve immediately with the garnishes arranged around the edge of the plate.

Note: If you have raw shrimp and squid, quickly stir-fry them in a little oil until cooked, then set aside until needed.

Alternatives & Variations
- The tops of spring onion (scallion) can be used instead of garlic chives.
- Use just one type of noodles.
- This dish can also be made with sliced pork or chicken. Stir-fry in a little oil over high heat and remove before frying the garlic. Return to the wok in place of the shrimp and squid.
- Use a commercial chilli paste (sambal oelek) or chilli sauce.

 Dhal [Lentil Purée]

Dhal is an excellent accompaniment to Tandoori Chicken, Naan and Mint Chutney.

Ingredients

1 tablespoon ghee
1 medium onion, finely chopped
1 teaspoon fresh ginger, minced
1 garlic clove, minced
½ teaspoon ground turmeric
½ cup (3½ oz/100 g) yellow or red lentils, soaked for 5 hours then rinsed and drained
2½ cups (18 fl oz/550 ml) hot water or more
1 medium potato, cut into large pieces
¼ teaspoon garam masala
½ teaspoon salt

SERVES 4

Method

Heat the ghee over medium-low heat, add the onion, ginger and garlic and fry until the onion is lightly coloured.

Add the turmeric and stir until combined. Add the lentils and fry for 1 minute.

Add the hot water, stir well then reduce the heat to low, cover and simmer for 20 minutes.

Add the potato, cover again and continue to simmer until the potato is cooked. If you prefer thinner dhal add extra water during this stage. Stir in the garam masala and salt.

 Mint Chutney

This very easy mint chutney is an excellent accompaniment to Tandoori Chicken, Naan and Dhal. It is best made close to serving as it can discolour and separate if stored for too long.

Ingredients

¾ cup mint leaves, firmly packed
2 tablespoons lemon juice
1 shallot segment, roughly sliced
¼ teaspoon garam masala
1 medium green chilli, seeded and roughly chopped
1 tablespoon water
1 teaspoon sugar
¼ teaspoon salt

MAKES ABOUT ½ CUP/4 FL OZ/60 ML

Method

Place all of the ingredients in a blender or food processor and blend until smooth.

Baby Choi Sum with Oyster Sauce

This delicious vegetable is an excellent accompaniment to any Chinese-style meal. Other Asian greens can also be prepared in this way although some varieties may take a little longer to cook.

Ingredients

½ teaspoon salt
1 teaspoon peanut oil
1 bunch baby choi sum, thoroughly washed and ends trimmed
¼ cup (2 fl oz/60 ml) oyster sauce
¼ cup (2 fl oz/60 ml) Chicken Stock (*see* recipe)

SERVES 4 AS A SIDE DISH

Method

Bring a large pan or wok of water (three-quarters full) to the boil. Add the salt and peanut oil. Reduce the heat to low so that the water is just simmering.

Add the choi sum and push it gently under the water. Put on a lid and cook for 2 minutes.

Meanwhile, mix together the oyster sauce and chicken stock. Lift the choi sum out of the water with a pair of tongs, drain and arrange it on a large platter. Drizzle with the oyster sauce mixture and serve immediately.

Naan and Garlic Naan [Indian Leavened Bread]

Adding sweetened condensed milk to the recipe makes a light and fluffy naan. The best results are obtained when it is cooked in a Tandoori oven. However since few of us are lucky enough to have one, I have adapted the recipe for cooking in a frying pan and on a grill, using instant dried yeast.

Ingredients

1 tablespoon sweetened condensed milk
¾ cup (6 fl oz/175 ml) tepid water
1 teaspoon instant dried yeast
¼ teaspoon salt
9 oz (250 g) plain (all-purpose) flour, plus
    extra for dusting
1 tablespoon vegetable oil
Water, for brushing
Melted ghee, for brushing
Finely chopped garlic (optional)

MAKES 6

Method

Mix together the condensed milk and water in a small bowl. In a large bowl, mix together the yeast, salt and flour then add the condensed milk mixture. Mix to a soft, sticky dough for about 2 minutes.

Add the oil and knead into the dough with your fist for 2 minutes until the dough is soft and slightly wet. Cover with plastic wrap (cling film) and leave for 2–3 hours until well risen.

Punch down (knock back) and knead until smooth on a lightly floured surface.

Divide into 6 pieces. On a well-floured surface, roll a piece into a smooth ball between your palms then flatten with your hand and roll into a circle or oblong about ⅛ in (3–4 mm) thick.

Turn on the grill (broiler) to high and leave to heat up. Meanwhile, heat a heavy pan or an electric frying-pan to medium hot. When the pan is hot, flip the naan from one hand to the other to remove any excess flour, brush one side with water and place wet side down into the pan.

Cook for about 3 minutes until the underside is light golden and easy to remove. If any large air bubbles form, prick them with a skewer.

Transfer to the hot grill, keeping it at medium distance from the heat, and grill (broil) until slightly puffed and speckled with brown spots. Prick any large air bubbles.

Remove and brush lightly with ghee and wrap in a clean dish towel or aluminium foil until ready to serve.

Alternatives & Variations
• For Garlic Naan, roll the ball of dough into a circle about 4¾ in (12 cm) in diameter. Sprinkle with garlic, fold in 4 sides and form another smooth ball between your palms. Rest the dough for a few minutes and then roll again and cook as for plain naan.

Roti Canai [Flatbread with Curry Sauce]

Roti Canai (pronounced 'ro-tee chanai') is a very popular and extremely delicious breakfast dish found throughout Malaysia, Singapore and Southern Thailand. It is similar to Indian paratha though it is lighter and crisper. The dough is often filled with egg or banana and drizzled with sweetened condensed milk or sometimes it is filled with a savoury meat mixture to make a delicious pastry called murtabak. However when fried without any filling and served with dhal or curry sauce it is called Roti Canai. The curry sauce is sometimes taken from a curry that has been made with a spice paste and coconut milk.

Ingredients

1 egg
1 cup (8 fl oz/250 ml) warm water
1 teaspoon salt
1 lb 6 oz (600 g) plain (all-purpose) flour,
   plus extra for dusting
½ teaspoon sugar
Vegetable oil or ghee

To Serve
Curry sauce

Makes about 12

Method

Whisk together the egg, water and salt. Sieve the flour into a bowl, add the sugar and mix in enough liquid to form a soft dough.

Turn onto a floured surface and knead for at least 5 minutes until smooth. Divide into 12 and form each piece into a ball. Coat each ball with oil or melted ghee. Place on a large plate (but keep the balls separate), cover with plastic wrap (cling film) and leave in a cool but unrefrigerated place overnight. In warm weather, let stand for only 3–4 hours.

Pour some oil or melted ghee into a small bowl. Dip a ball of dough into the oil, place on a clean bench and, using your hands, flatten the ball until you have a circle about 15 cm (6 in) in diameter.

Now pick up the bottom right section of the circle with your right hand. Use the fingers of your left hand to steady the dough as you quickly pick up the whole piece of dough and flick it forwards and slap it down on the surface. You will find that the dough stretches. (Note: this is quite tricky and requires some practice!) Repeat (rotating the dough a little as you go) until the circle is paper thin and quite large, you can smoothen out any thick parts with oiled fingers. Don't worry if there are a few holes.

FOLDING METHOD
You need a large hotplate to use this method. Place the large piece of paper-thin dough in a large preheated oiled hotplate and quickly fold the four sides into the middle. Fry for 2–3 minutes, turn over and fry the other side until the roti is crisp and golden.

COIL METHOD
Gather and roughly pleat the dough into a long sausage shape then twist it into a coil and tuck the 'tail' under. Use a rolling pin to roll it out flat into a circle about 3–4mm thick. Fry for 2–3 minutes on each side in a large preheated oiled pan until crisp and golden. Place the finished rotis in a warm oven (wrapped in foil) while making the rest.

TO SERVE
Serve the rotis with a small side dish of curry sauce.

Cendol [Shaved Ice with Green Rice-Flour Noodles, Palm-Sugar Syrup and Coconut Milk]

Cendol (pronounced 'chendol') is a deliciously refreshing concoction that could be described as a dessert, snack or drink. It is very popular in Malaysia and variations of it can also be found in Indonesia and Thailand.

Ingredients

2 cups crushed ice
4 tablespoons Palm-Sugar Syrup (*see below*)
1 tablespoon canned red kidney beans, rinsed and drained
1 tablespoon Green Rice-Flour Noodles (*see below*)
1 cup (8 fl oz/250 ml) coconut milk

Green Rice-Flour Noodles
½ cup (1¾ oz/50 g) rice flour
1 cup (8 fl oz/250 ml) water
2 teaspoons pandan extract
1 teaspoon sugar

Palm-Sugar Syrup
¼ cup (1 ½ oz/45 g) palm sugar, shaved or grated
¼ cup (2 fl oz/60 ml) water

Serves 2

Method

Green Rice-Flour Noodles
Place the rice flour and water in a small pan and mix to a smooth paste.

Add the pandan extract and sugar. Stir over low heat until thick.

Place a colander (or a sieve with large holes) over a bowl of cold water. Push the rice-flour mixture through the holes into the water to make the noodles.

Leave them in the water for a few minutes then drain and place in the coconut milk until ready to serve.

Palm-Sugar Syrup
Place the palm sugar and water in a small pan over medium heat.

Bring it to the boil and boil for 2 minutes until syrupy. Set aside.

To Serve
Place a cup of ice in each of 2 serving bowls. Drizzle 2 tablespoons of syrup over each.

Add 1 tablespoon of red kidney beans and 1 tablespoon of noodles to each bowl.

Pour ½ cup (4 fl oz/125 ml) coconut milk into each bowl and serve immediately.

Alternatives & Variations
• Use soft brown sugar instead of palm sugar.
• Use a few drops of green food colouring and vanilla essence instead of pandan extract.

Flaky Egg Custard Tarts

These light, vanilla-flavoured little tarts are found in all dim sum restaurants and, for me, no dim sum meal is complete without them!

Ingredients

PASTRY
9 oz (250 g) plain (all-purpose) flour
Pinch of salt
4½ oz (125 g) margarine, chilled
2½ oz (75 g) vegetable shortening, chilled
1 egg, lightly beaten
½ teaspoon vanilla extract
1 teaspoon lemon juice
4–5 tablespoons iced water or enough to make a fairly firm dough

FILLING
⅔ cup (¼ pint/150 ml) water
⅔ cup (4¼ oz/130 g) sugar
4 eggs
⅓ cup (2½ oz/75 ml) evaporated milk
Seeds of 1 vanilla bean (pod)

MAKES ABOUT 24

Method

PASTRY
Sieve the flour and salt into a large bowl. Quickly grate (shred) in the margarine and shortening and toss to coat with flour. Work gently with your fingertips to ensure that there are no large clumps of fat.

Make a well in the centre and add the egg, vanilla extract, lemon juice and water. Mix with a knife until the dough just comes together.

Turn onto a floured board and knead gently until smooth.

Roll the pastry to a large rectangle about 0.5 cm (⅛ in) thick. Fold the top third into the centre and the bottom third up so that you have three layers. Repeat this rolling and folding twice more then seal in a plastic bag and refrigerate for at least 1 hour.

FILLING
Place the water and sugar in a small pan. Stir over low heat until the sugar has dissolved then allow to cool.

Place the eggs in a large bowl and beat to break up the yolks. Add the cooled mixture, evaporated milk and vanilla seeds and beat until well combined and smooth.

TARTS
Preheat the oven to 220°C/425°F/Gas mark 7. Lightly grease 2 x 12 cup patty pans (tins).

On a floured surface, roll the pastry to 3–4 mm (⅛ in) thick. Stamp out rounds and use to line the prepare pans.

Line each with paper and baking beans and bake blind for 10 minutes. Remove the paper cases and rice and bake again for 5 minutes.

Reduce the temperature to 160°C/325°F/Gas mark 3.

Pour the filling into the pastry cases. Bake for about 20 minutes, or until the custard is just set.

Cool on a wire rack. Serve fresh.

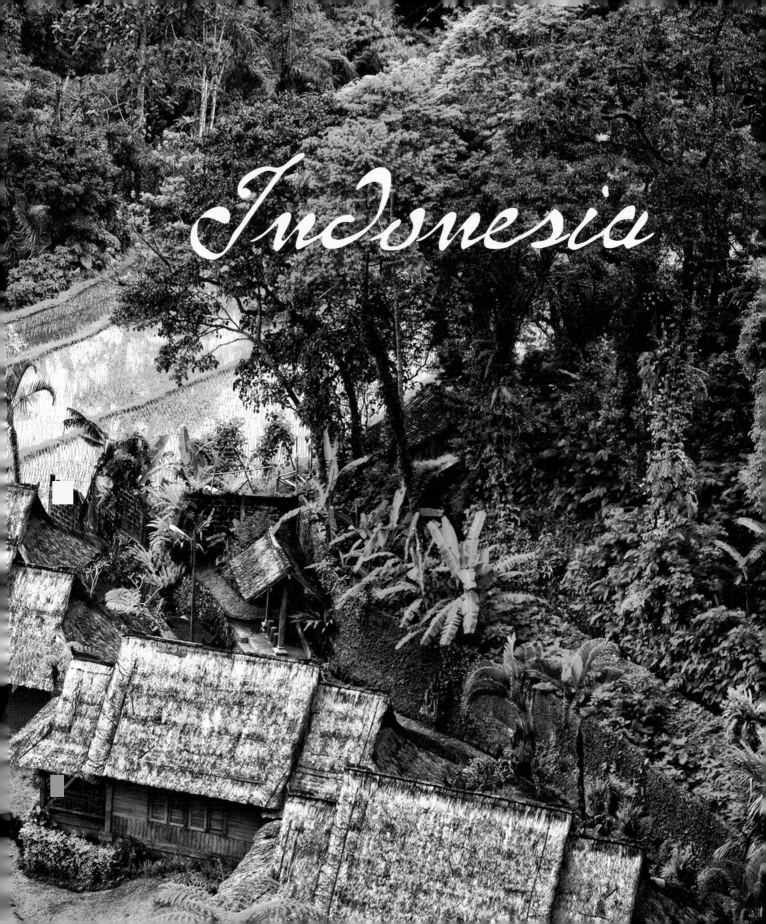

Indonesia

Indonesia — Introduction

In Indonesia we find a wide diversity of cuisine not only influenced by the many hundreds of years of Indian traders, Chinese migrants and Dutch rule, but also by the more simple things such as the availability of ingredients, religion, and time-honoured island traditions.

Throughout the thousands of islands that make up the Indonesian archipelago you will find some common (mainly Javanese) dishes such as Nasi Goreng (fried rice), Mee Goreng (fried noodles), Gado-Gado (vegetables with peanut sauce) and Kare Ayam (chicken curry), to name just a few. However the myriad ethnic groups such as Balinese, Javanese, Sasak or Batak etc. have their own unique dishes and distinctive culinary flavours.

Traditional Balinese food tends to be very aromatic. Common ingredients include grated coconut, lime juice, shallots and fragrant spice pastes (bumbu). These spice pastes form the basis of many dishes and are usually made of various combinations of chillies, garlic, ginger, galangal, turmeric, kencur, shallots and terasi (a very pungent paste made from dried shrimp).

The Sasak foods of Lombok are usually very spicy, containing lots of cabe rawit (bird's eye chillies). Other staple ingredients include garlic, ginger, shallots, galangal and terasi.

Sumatra features a very wide range of foods and flavours, from the northern Babi Panggang (roast pork with a sauce containing pig's blood) and the special freshwater fish dishes of Samosir Island (an island in the middle of Lake Toba) to the spicy foods found in western Sumatra. The food known as Masakan Padang or Minangkabau includes the famous Rendang (a dry and spicy slow-cooked coconut milk–based curry). Padang food restaurants can be found all over Indonesia.

Indonesian people generally eat whenever they are hungry rather than at set times of the day. In many Indonesian towns and villages a lot of cooking is done in the morning. A whole day's food is often prepared in the morning: a big pot of rice is cooked and family members help themselves during the day.

Indonesian food is perhaps best experienced when served as a rijstafel (rice table). Here small amounts of dishes and sambals are served with plain rice. This is a great opportunity to sample many of the country's delicious foods.

Sate Ayam [Chicken Satay]

Satays (grilled skewered meat or fish with peanut sauce) are one of the most popular dishes in Indonesia. Many variations are found throughout Southeast Asia. This recipe is a Sumatran version and is quite spicy so for a milder sauce, reduce the number of chillies.

Ingredients

12 bamboo skewers
1 lb 2 oz (500 g) boneless chicken (thighs or breast), cut into bite-sized pieces
1 tablespoon margarine
½ teaspoon salt
¼ teaspoon white pepper
2 teaspoons lemon juice

Satay Sauce

½ cup (4 fl oz/125 ml) vegetable oil
½ cup (2½ oz/75 g) raw peanuts with skins
3 shallot segments (about 1½ tablespoons), roughly sliced
2 medium garlic cloves, peeled and roughly sliced
3 small long red chillies or 1 large long red chilli
7 green bird's eye chillies
1 teaspoon salt
³/₈ in (1 cm) piece kencur
2 tablespoons palm sugar
½ cup (4 fl oz/125 ml) hot water

Makes 12 or more satays

Method

Preparation

Soak 12 bamboo skewers in cold water for at least 30 minutes to prevent burning.

Mix the chicken pieces with the margarine, ½ teaspoon salt, pepper and lemon juice and set aside while making the sauce.

Satay Sauce

Heat the oil in a wok over medium heat and fry the peanuts for about 2–3 minutes, or until light golden brown taking care not to burn them. Remove and drain.

In the same oil, fry the shallots for 30 seconds then add the garlic. Fry for about 1½ minutes, or until golden and slightly crisp. Remove and drain.

Using a mortar and pestle, grind the chillies with 1 teaspoon of salt. Add the garlic, shallots and kencur and grind again until well combined.

Add the peanuts and continue grinding until you have a lumpy paste.

Add the palm sugar and grind again until well combined. At this stage, the satay paste can be stored in the refrigerator for up to 1 week.

Transfer to a bowl and stir in the hot water. Add more water if you prefer a thinner sauce.

Satays

Thread 3 or 4 pieces of chicken onto each skewer. Grill (broil) over coals (not too hot) for about 30 minutes or until cooked, turning occasionally.

To serve, spoon the sauce over each satay and serve the remaining sauce on the side.

Alternatives & Variations
- Onion can be used instead of shallots.
- Substitute green chillies for the bird's eye chillies. If you want a milder flavour, use only 2 or 3 of them and remove the seeds and membrane.

Pepes Ikan [Grilled Fish Wrapped in Banana Leaf]

Pepes Ikan simply consists of pieces of fish mixed with a Balinese spice paste, wrapped in a banana leaf and grilled (broiled) over hot coals. It is a very popular dish in Bali.

Ingredients

14 oz (400 g) of any firm-fleshed fish
   fillets, cut into bite-sized chunks
Salt and white pepper, to taste
2 teaspoons Balinese spice paste (Bumbu
   Bali Ketut, *see* recipe)
2 teaspoons coconut or peanut oil
Pinch of chicken seasoning powder
   (optional)
Banana leaves or tin foil, cut into
   4 squares each 8 in (20 cm)
Small pieces of bamboo sticks or split
   cocktail sticks

To Serve
Plain rice
A wedge of lemon
Jukut Urab (*see* recipe)

Serves 2–4

Method

Mix together the fish, salt, pepper, Balinese spice paste, oil and chicken powder.

Using three layers of banana leaf or foil, place one quarter of the fish mixture on the bottom third of each banana leaf or foil square. Fold over and roll into a parcel.

Secure each end of the banana leaf with small pieces of bamboo stick or split toothpicks. If using foil, fold the ends in to enclose the fish.

Grill (broil) over hot coals for 5 minutes on each side.

Serve with plain rice, a wedge of lemon and a Balinese vegetable dish such as Jukut Urab.

Alternatives & Variations
• The parcels can also be steamed.

Sate Lilit Babi

[Grilled Pork Mince Satay with Balinese Spice Paste and Coconut]

These Balinese specialties make a delicious entrée or can be served as part of a shared meal. Lilit means 'to twist'; traditionally the mince mixture is twisted around the bamboo stick. Note that twisting is only possible if you can get flat bamboo skewers, as it will not work with the round ones!

Ingredients

6 bamboo skewers
6 oz (175 g) pork, finely minced
1½ teaspoons Balinese spice paste
   (Bumbu Bali Ketut, *see* recipe)
1½ tablespoons freshly grated (shredded)
   coconut
½ teaspoon lime juice
½ teaspoon palm sugar, grated
   (shredded)
Salt and pepper, to taste
Pinch chicken seasoning powder
   (optional)

TO SERVE
Sambal Kecap (*see* recipe)

MAKES 6

Method

Soak the bamboo skewers in cold water for at least 30 minutes to prevent burning.

Process the pork mince in a food processor to a very fine consistency.

Mix all of the ingredients until very well combined with your hands.

Take about ¾ tablespoon of mince mixture and press around the top 2 in (4–5 cm) of the skewer tapering in at the base like a chicken drumstick.

Grill (broil) for about 10 minutes under high heat, turning 3 or 4 times. Serve with Sambal Kecap.

Alternatives & Variations
• Use lemon juice instead of lime juice.
• Use soft brown sugar instead of palm sugar.
• Use 1 tablespoon of desiccated (dry shredded, unsweetened) coconut instead of fresh coconut. Soak in hot water for 5 minutes then strain and squeeze out as much liquid as possible.
• Use minced chicken instead of pork.

Ikan Panggang Tinombur

[Whole Grilled Fish with a Spicy Candle Nut Paste]

This dish is a specialty of the villages on the shores of Lake Toba in Northern Sumatra. It is traditionally made with fresh lake fish called ikan nila, however bream or snapper can be used. The spice paste contains an unusual spice called andaliman or intir-intir. This spice appears to be unique to the area and is widely used there. It is a small greenish-black berry the same size as a peppercorn and has a lemony peppery flavour. If eaten raw it will numb the lips! As it is not readily available unless you live in Sumatra I suggest lemongrass and black pepper as a substitute.

Ingredients

1 whole, cleaned fish, weighing about
   1¾ lb (1 kg)

SPICE PASTE
9 medium shallot segments, unpeeled
1¾ in (4 cm) piece fresh ginger, unpeeled
3 garlic cloves, unpeeled
12 candle nuts, roughly chopped
7–10 green bird's eye chillies
4 medium or 2 large long red chillies
1 teaspoon salt
1½ teaspoons lemongrass, finely chopped
½ teaspoon ground black pepper
1 teaspoon lemon juice, to taste
2 tablespoons hot water

TO SERVE
Plain rice

SERVES 2

Method

FISH
Place the fish in a grilling (broiling) basket and grill (broil) slowly for about 1 hour or until cooked, turning a few times. Meanwhile, prepare the spice paste.

SPICE PASTE
Grill the shallots, ginger and garlic until the skins start to blacken. Set aside and peel when cool enough to handle.

Dry-fry the candle nuts in a hot pan or wok, stirring constantly for 2–3 minutes, or until well toasted.

Place the chillies and salt in a mortar or grinding stone and grind to a paste.

Add the lemongrass, pepper, candle nuts and ginger, grinding to a paste after each addition.

Finally add the garlic and shallots and grind again until the paste is fairly smooth.

Transfer to a bowl and add the lemon juice and hot water. Mix well.

TO SERVE
Test the fish by inserting a knife into the flesh along the backbone. If it parts easily and is no longer opaque, it is cooked.

Place it on a serving dish and spread the paste over the entire surface. Serve any extra spice paste on the side along with plain rice.

Alternatives & Variations
• Brown or white onions can be used instead of shallots.
• Substitute 16 raw macadamia nuts or 30 blanched raw almonds for candle nuts.
• For a milder spice paste, remove the seeds and membrane of the chillies.

Ikan Naneura [Fish Marinated in Spices, Peanuts and Lemon Juice]

This dish is traditionally made with lake goldfish (carp), however any variety of very fresh, soft-textured fish can be used. The fish are split open and the bones removed and then the flesh is covered with a peanut spice paste and lots of lemon juice. The acid in the lemon 'cooks' the fish.

Ingredients

2 whole, cleaned (or filleted) fresh, soft-textured fish, weighing about 1 lb 6 oz (600 g) each
2 tablespoons hot water
1¼ cups (½ pint/300 ml) lemon juice

PEANUT SPICE PASTE
½ cup (2 oz/60 g) raw peanuts with skins
¼ cup (1 oz/30 g) candle nuts
3 teaspoons coriander seeds
4 shallot segments, halved
1¼ in (3 cm) piece fresh ginger, peeled and cut into thirds
2 small garlic cloves, peeled
½ in (1.5 cm) piece fresh turmeric, peeled and cut in half
8 green bird's eye chillies
1 large long red chilli
½ teaspoon salt
1 teaspoon lemongrass, finely chopped
¼ teaspoon ground black pepper
¼ cup (2 fl oz/60 ml) hot water
1 cup (8 fl oz/250 ml) lemon juice

TO SERVE
Plain rice
Vegetables/salad

SERVES 4

Method

Slice the fish horizontally along the backbone and through the head. Open out butterfly-style and remove the gills and bones. Use tweezers to remove any small bones and cut off the fins. Refrigerate until needed

PEANUT SPICE PASTE
Heat a wok over medium-low heat, add the peanuts and dry-fry, stirring continuously for about 2–3 minutes until well toasted and the skins are slightly blackened. Remove and set aside. Repeat the process with the candle nuts and then dry-fry the coriander seeds for 1 minute.

Dry-fry the shallots, ginger, garlic and turmeric together for 2–3 minutes until slightly charred and softened. On a large grinding stone or mortar and pestle, grind the chillies and salt to a paste. Add the turmeric, candle nuts, coriander seeds, lemongrass and pepper, grinding well after each addition.

Add the ginger, garlic and shallots and grind again. Finally add the peanuts and continue to grind until you have a thick, lumpy paste. Add a little water if necessary.

Transfer to a bowl and mix in the hot water and lemon juice.

FISH
Place the fish in a non-metallic dish. Pour 1 tablespoon of hot water over each fish then pour over the lemon juice mixture. Spread the spice paste over the fish ensuring that all flesh is covered. Cover with plastic wrap (cling film) and refrigerate for at least 8 hours.

Place the fish on a serving dish and spoon over some of the marinade. Serve with plain rice and vegetables or salad.

Alternatives & Variations
• Brown or white onions can be used instead of shallots.
• Substitute raw macadamia nuts or blanched raw almonds for candle nuts.
• For a milder spice paste, remove the seeds and membrane of the chillies.
• ½ teaspoon ground turmeric can be substituted for fresh turmeric.

Sambal Ikan Teri [Crispy Anchovies with Peanuts and Chilli]

Ikan Teri literally means 'anchovies', but is also the common name used to refer to this sambal, which is delicious served alone or with plain rice. It is commonly found as part of Nasi Lemak, a Malaysian dish of coconut rice, boiled egg, cucumber and a spicy chicken curry.

Ingredients

1 cup (8 fl oz/250 ml) vegetable oil, plus an extra 2 tablespoons
½ cup (2 oz/60 g) raw peanuts with skins
2 cups (4 oz/115 g) dried anchovies (ikan bilis)
1 quantity Chilli Paste (*see* below)
2 teaspoons sugar

CHILLI PASTE

4 small or 2 long red chillies
2 garlic cloves, peeled and roughly chopped
2 shallot segments (about 1 tablespoon), roughly chopped
2 small tomatoes, peeled and roughly chopped

SERVES 4 OR MORE

Method

CHILLI PASTE

Using a mortar and pestle, grind the chillies finely. Add the garlic and shallots and grind again. Add the tomatoes and continue to grind until you have a fairly smooth paste.

SAMBAL

Heat the 2 cups (16 fl oz/500 ml) of oil in a wok over medium-low heat and deep-fry the peanuts until golden brown, about 2 minutes, taking care not to overcook them. Remove the peanuts and drain.

Reheat the oil until hot, add the anchovies and fry for about 3–5 minutes, or until crisp. Remove the anchovies and drain.

In a clean wok or pan, heat the extra 2 tablespoons of oil over medium-high heat. Add the Chilli Paste and sugar, and fry for 2 minutes, stirring constantly.

Toss in the drained peanuts and anchovies and stir-fry until well mixed.

> ### Alternatives & Variations
> • Brown or white onion can be used instead of shallots.
> • For a milder flavour, remove the seeds and membrane of the chillies.
> • To make a delicious finger snack to accompany drinks, use only about ¼ of the Chilli Paste. This will make a drier sambal that can easily be eaten with the fingers. Alternatively, just mix together the fried peanuts and anchovies without the sambal for an equally delicious snack.

Kare Ayam [Indonesian Chicken Curry]

This easy Indonesian curry recipe is very quick to make as it uses leftover chicken. The curry paste is available at most Asian food stores. Alternatively, with just a little extra work, you can make your own.

Ingredients

1 tablespoon coconut or peanut oil
1½ tablespoons Balinese spice paste
  (Bumbu Bali Ketut, *see* recipe)
1 x 1¼ oz (35 g) packet bumbu kare
  ayam (Indonesian curry paste)
1 cup (8 fl oz/250 ml) coconut milk
11 oz (300 g) cooked chicken, cut into
  bite-sized strips

TO SERVE
Plain rice

SERVES 4 AS PART OF A SHARED MEAL

Method

Heat the wok over medium-low heat and add the oil. Fry the spice paste and curry paste together for 1 minute.

Add the coconut milk, stir and bring to the boil.

Add the chicken, increase the heat to high and cook, stirring almost constantly, for 2 minutes. Serve with plain rice.

 *Ayam Bali* [Balinese Chicken]

This delicious and delicately flavoured dish

Ingredients

1 small chicken, weighing about 1¾ lb
  (1 kg)
2 cups (16 fl oz/500 ml) water
1 stalk lemongrass, bruised and tied
  in a knot
1 salam leaf

MARINADE
1 peanut-sized piece shrimp paste,
  toasted over a gas flame or wrapped in
  foil and lightly toasted over an electric
  element
1 walnut-sized piece tamarind pulp
1 tablespoon soy sauce (kecap asin)
½ teaspoon salt
¼ teaspoon black pepper
1 tablespoon coconut or peanut oil

SPICE PASTE
4 shallot segments (about 2 tablespoons),
  roughly sliced
5 garlic cloves, peeled and roughly sliced
1 large red chilli, seeded and sliced
1¾ in (4 cm) piece fresh turmeric
1¾ in (4 cm) piece fresh ginger
3 candle nuts, roughly chopped
¼ teaspoon salt

TO SERVE
Plain rice

SERVES 2

Method

MARINADE AND SPICE PASTE
Mix together the marinade ingredients. Rub all over chicken, inside and outside and marinate for at least 15 minutes.

Make the spice paste by grinding the ingredients in a mortar until you have a thick paste.

CHICKEN
Put the chicken and marinade in a pot; add the spice paste, water, lemongrass and salam leaf.

Bring to the boil then cover the pot, reduce heat to low and simmer for 1 hour.

TO SERVE
Remove the chicken and divide into serving portions. Place in a serving dish and pour some or all of the flavoured liquid over. Serve with plain rice.

Alternatives & Variations
- A bay leaf may be substituted for salam leaf.
- 1 teaspoon tamarind concentrate may be substituted for pulp.
- Light soy sauce may be substituted for kecap asin but add more salt if necessary.
- 1½ teaspoons ground turmeric can be substituted for fresh turmeric.
- 3 macadamia nuts or 6 blanched almonds can be substituted for candle nuts.
- Make the spice paste in a food processor.

Pelecing Ayam [Spicy Grilled Chicken]

Hot, spicy and sweet, this chicken dish is best served with plain rice and a cooling drink.

Ingredients

1 small chicken, weighing about 1 lb
  (1¾ kg), halved or butterflied
¼ teaspoon salt
¼ teaspoon pepper

CHILLI SAUCE
2 large red chillies, seeded and chopped
8–15 red bird's eye chillies (depending
  on desired spiciness)
5 garlic cloves, peeled and roughly
  chopped
¼ teaspoon salt
1 tablespoon coconut or peanut oil
½ chicken stock cube mixed with ½ cup
  (4 fl oz/125 ml) hot water

TO SERVE
Plain rice
1 cucumber, peeled and sliced into sticks

SERVES 2 OR 3

Method

Wash and dry the chicken and either place in a wire barbecue basket or insert a skewer or skewers through the width of the chicken to keep it flat. Rub with the salt and pepper.

Grill over hot coals for 30–45 minutes or until cooked, turning 4 or 5 times. Prepare the Chilli Sauce while the chicken is grilling (broiling).

CHILLI SAUCE
Grind the chillies, garlic and ¼ teaspoon salt to a paste on a grinding stone or in a mortar.

Heat a wok over medium-low heat and add the oil. Add the chilli paste, increase heat to medium and fry, stirring constantly, for 1 minute.

Stir in the combined chicken stock cube and water and cook for another minute. Turn off the heat until the chicken is ready.

TO SERVE
When the chicken is cooked, cut it into quarters or eighths, add it to the wok and toss in the sauce over medium heat until well coated.

Serve with plain rice and cucumber sticks.

Babi Kecap [Balinese Sweet Soy Pork]

This dish could be described as a healthy version of sweet and sour pork. It is quick and easy and delicious.

Ingredients

1 tablespoon coconut or peanut oil

2 tablespoons garlic, peeled and thinly sliced

½ cup shallot segments, sliced

2 long red chillies, seeded and thickly sliced diagonally

2 tomatoes, halved and cut into wedges

1¾ in (4 cm) piece galangal, cut in half and pounded with a mallet

¼ cup celery leaves, roughly chopped

½ teaspoon ground nutmeg

½ teaspoon salt

¼ teaspoon pepper

12 oz (350 g) pork fillet, thinly sliced and pounded with a mallet

2 tablespoons sweet soy sauce (kecap manis)

To Serve

Plain rice

Serves 2

Method

Heat a wok over medium-low heat and add the oil.

Add the garlic and shallots and fry for about 2 minutes, stirring almost constantly until softened and lightly coloured. Add the chillies, tomatoes, galangal and celery leaves and stir.

Add the nutmeg, salt, pepper and pork. Stir, then add the kecap manis.

Stir well, cover and cook very slowly for 20 minutes. Serve with plain rice.

Alternatives & Variations
• Use a ¾ in (2 cm) piece of fresh ginger instead of galangal.

Rendang Daging [Quick Beef Rendang]

This is a beef rendang recipe with a difference! Unlike the traditional rendang, which take hours to cook, this version only takes 30 minutes (excluding making the Rendang Paste and toasted coconut). It also incorporates vegetables, which is a little different to the traditional rendang.

Ingredients

RENDANG PASTE

2 teaspoons coriander seeds

2 cardamom pods

1 whole star anise

¾ in (2 cm) piece fresh ginger, chopped

3 teaspoons galangal, chopped

2 garlic cloves, peeled and roughly chopped

5 shallot segments (about 3 tablespoons), roughly chopped

4 large red chillies, seeded and chopped

2 red bird's eye chillies, chopped

2 candle nuts

2 tablespoons coconut or peanut oil

KELAPA GORENG

½ cup (2 oz/60 g) fresh coconut, finely grated (shredded)

Method

KELAPA GORENG

Place the grated coconut in a dry pan or wok over very low heat and cook, stirring occasionally at first, and more frequently when it starts to change colour. This will take at least 1 hour.

Once the coconut is dark brown, place it in a mortar or spice grinder and grind to a thick paste.

Kelapa Goreng will keep for weeks when stored in a screw-top jar in the pantry, so it is worthwhile making a larger quantity.

RENDANG PASTE

Toast the coriander seeds, cardamom pods and star anise in a dry wok, stirring over low heat for 4–5 minutes, or until aromatic. (Note: the extra cardamom pods and star anise for the curry can be also toasted here, then removed and set aside for later).

Transfer the Rendang Paste spices to a mortar or spice grinder, cool and then grind to a fine powder.

Add the remaining Rendang Paste ingredients (except the oil) and continue to grind until you have a thick paste.

Note: As you only need 2 tablespoons of Rendang Paste for the recipe, at this stage the excess can be frozen in portions. Alternatively fry the Rendang Paste in the 2 tablespoons of oil for 3–4 minutes until aromatic and oily. Any excess can be stored in the refrigerator for up to 1 month.

Recipe continues

Rendang

2 tablespoons Rendang Paste (*see* above)
9 oz (250 g) beef (round steak or similar),
  thinly sliced
1¼ cups (½ pint/300 ml) water
2 stalks lemongrass, bruised and tied in
  a knot
3 cardamom pods, toasted
½ whole star anise, toasted
1 salam leaf
3 red or green bird's eye chillies, sliced
  (optional)
1 large potato, cubed and half-cooked
1 medium carrot, sliced and half-cooked
1½–2 cups (12–16 fl oz/350–475 ml)
  coconut cream
Salt and pepper, to taste
½ teaspoon sugar
¼ teaspoon lemon juice
½ cup (3 oz/85 g) green (French) beans,
  cut into 1 in (2.5 cm) lengths
½ tablespoon Kelapa Goreng

Garnish
2 teaspoons chopped celery leaves
  (optional)
2 teaspoons crispy fried shallots
  (optional)

To Serve
Plain rice

Serves 2 or 3

Rendang

Heat a wok over medium heat. If using freshly made or frozen Rendang Paste, fry it in the 2 tablespoons of oil for 3–4 minutes until aromatic. If using Rendang Paste that has already been fried add it to the dry wok and fry for 5 seconds.

Add the beef and stir-fry over high heat for 30 seconds. Add the water and stir.

Add the lemongrass, cardamom pods, star anise, salam leaf and bird's eye chillies (if using). Stir and cook over high heat for 15 minutes until the water has evaporated. If it looks too dry toward the end, either reduce the heat or add a little more water.

Add the potato, carrot, coconut cream, salt, pepper and sugar. Stir and cook for 8 minutes over high heat.

Stir in the lemon juice and green beans. Add the Kelapa Goreng and stir well.

Lower the heat to medium-low and cook for another 10 minutes, stirring regularly, until it is fairly dry and the oil rises to the top. Add some extra coconut cream or milk during this stage if the rendang seems too dry or if you prefer more sauce.

Remove the lemongrass, cardamom and star anise before serving. Garnish with chopped celery leaves and crispy fried shallots. Serve with plain rice.

Alternatives & Variations
- Use 2 macadamia nuts or 4 blanched almonds or 2 heaped teaspoons ground almonds instead of candle nuts.
- Use a small bay leaf or curry leaf instead of a salam leaf or omit it altogether.
- The Kelapa Goreng can be omitted without making too much difference.
- Make the Rendang Paste in a food processor or electric blender. If necessary, add 1 or 2 tablespoons of water to assist blending.
- Make a double or triple quantity of paste to freeze.
- Make extra Kelapa Goreng to store.
- Use a commercial beef rendang paste and disregard the packet instructions. The above method should give a better end result.
- This dish can also be made with chicken.
- Rendang can also be made without potatoes, carrots and beans.

Gado-Gado [Mixed Vegetables with Peanut Sauce]

Gado-Gado can be made with virtually any mix of vegetables. The tofu and/or tempe are not essential to this recipe.

Ingredients

1 cup (8 oz/225 g) tofu, cut into ¾ in (2 cm) cubes
¾ cup (3 oz/85 g) tempeh, cut into ¾ in (2 cm) cubes
2 medium potatoes, cubed
1 carrot, sliced
2 cups (10 oz/280 g) green (French) beans, cut into 2 in (5 cm) lengths
3 cups (12 oz/350 g) Chinese cabbage or white cabbage, roughly chopped

Peanut Sauce

1 cup (4 oz/115 g) raw peanuts, skins on
½ cup (2 oz/60 g) coconut or vegetable oil, for frying the peanuts, tofu and tempe
4 green bird's eye chillies
1¼ in (3 cm) piece kencur
½ teaspoon kaffir lime zest
3 garlic cloves, peeled and roughly chopped
1 teaspoon salt
2½ tablespoons palm sugar
¾ cup (6 fl oz/175 ml) water
1 teaspoon light soy sauce

Serves 4 or more as a side dish

Method

Peanut Sauce

Grind the chillies, kencur, kaffir lime zest, garlic and salt to a paste with a mortar and pestle.

Heat the oil in a wok over medium-low heat. Fry the peanuts for about 2 minutes or until light golden brown. The oil must not be too hot or the peanuts will be too dark. Drain, add to the ground spices and continue to grind until you have a lumpy paste.

Now add the palm sugar and grind again adding 2–3 tablespoons of cold water, if necessary, to make a thick moist paste.

Bring the water to the boil in a wok or small saucepan. Add the peanut paste and light soy sauce and boil for about 2 minutes until you have a thick sauce. Add more water if you prefer a thinner sauce.

Gado-Gado

Reheat the oil that was used to fry the peanuts and fry the tofu until golden then remove and drain.

Now fry the tempe until dark golden brown. Remove and drain.

Bring a pot of water to the boil, add the potatoes and carrot and boil for about 10 minutes or until nearly tender.

Add the beans and cook for 4 minutes then add the cabbage and cook for 2 more minutes. Drain.

Place the vegetables on a serving dish, pour the sauce over, top with the tofu and tempeh, and serve.

Alternatives & Variations
- Lime or lemon zest can be used instead of kaffir lime zest.
- Use a ³/₈ in (1 cm) piece of galangal instead of kencur.
- Use soft brown sugar instead of palm sugar.
- Slice 1 or 2 hard-boiled eggs on top of the vegetables then pour over the sauce.

Pergedel [Fried Potato, Garlic and Onion Patties]

Also known as perkedel or bergedel, these little patties can be found in Padang food restaurants throughout Indonesia. Padang restaurants are notable for their window displays where the food is prepared and set out on shelves. There are countless versions of Pergedel – this is a very simple recipe.

Ingredients

1 garlic clove, peeled and finely chopped
2 tablespoons onion, finely chopped
2 cups (1 lb 2 oz/500 g) mashed potatoes
Salt and pepper, to taste
1 egg, lightly beaten

SERVES 4 AS A SIDE DISH

Method

Mix together the garlic and onion.

Season the potatoes with salt and pepper and mix well.

Place a tablespoonful of potato in one hand, make a dent in the middle and place a teaspoonful of onion and garlic in it.

Now place another tablespoonful of potato on top and form into a ball or patty. Repeat with the remaining ingredients.

Heat the oil over medium-low heat until hot. Roll the patties in beaten egg and deep-fry for about 4 minutes or until golden and crisp. Drain on paper towels and serve hot or cold.

Kacang Bakar [Roasted Peanuts]

Unsalted roasted peanuts are indispensable in Southeast Asian cooking. If you are unable to buy them, you can roast your own.

Ingredients

9 oz (250 g) raw peanuts, preferably the
    small red-skinned variety

MAKES 1½ CUPS (9 OZ/250 G)

Method

Heat a wok over high heat. Add the peanuts and reduce the heat to medium-low.

Stir slowly and continuously until the skins are cracked and slightly blackened in places. This will take about 15–20 minutes. Leave the peanuts to cool in a shallow tray.

Rub handfuls of peanuts between your palms to remove the skins. The peanuts can be stored in an airtight container for several weeks.

Jukut Vrab [Mixed Vegetables with Coconut]

This is a great way to make fairly ordinary vegetables more appealing. Combined with grated (shredded) coconut, chilli and lime juice, they really do taste great.

Ingredients

½ cup (1½ oz/45 g) carrots, julienned

1 cup (5 oz/150 g) green (French) beans, cut into 2 in (5 cm) lengths

1 cup (4 oz/115 g) white cabbage, roughly chopped

1 cup (4 oz/115 g) green bean leaves or any type of Asian greens, roughly chopped

1½ cups (4½ oz/125 g) coconut, freshly grated

2 red bird's eye chillies, finely chopped

½ teaspoon lime juice

1 teaspoon lemongrass, finely chopped

Salt and pepper, to taste

1 tablespoon crispy fried shallots (available at Asian food stores)

2 teaspoons palm sugar, grated (shredded)

SERVES 4 AS A SIDE DISH

Method

Boil or steam the carrots and beans in a steamer over medium-high heat for 4 minutes. Add the white cabbage and cook for 2 minutes. Finally add the greens and cook for 1 minute. The vegetables should be tender but still crunchy.

Place the grated coconut in a large bowl. Drain the vegetables and add to the coconut.

Now add all of the remaining ingredients and mix well together.

Alternatives & Variations

• Substitute the above vegetables with similar ones that you have available. Be careful not to overcook the vegetables – they must be boiled or steamed until they are tender but still crunchy.

• Use ½ cup (1¼ oz/35 g) of desiccated (dry, unsweetened shredded) coconut instead of fresh. Cover with boiling water, leave for about 5 minutes then drain and squeeze out all excess water.

Mee Goreng [Indonesian Fried Noodles]

An excellent accompaniment to Mee Goreng is sambal asli, a very hot chilli sauce that can be found on just about every restaurant table in Indonesia. It is available from most Asian food stores.

Ingredients

2 large or 6 small krupuk (prawn crackers), optional

2 teaspoons sweet soy sauce (kecap manis)

1 teaspoon salty soy sauce (kecap asin)

1 teaspoon chilli sauce

Salt and pepper, to taste

2 eggs

2 packets of 2-minute noodles, cooked according to packet instructions and drained

1 tablespoon coconut or peanut oil

5 garlic cloves, peeled and roughly chopped

½ cup (3 oz/85 g) pork, finely chopped or sliced

2 bird's eye chillies, finely chopped

½ cup (1½ oz/35 g) carrot, julienned

½ cup (2 oz/60 g) white cabbage, shredded

2 cups (8 oz/225 g) Asian greens, cut into 1¾ in (4 cm) slices

SERVES 2

Method

If using uncooked krupuk, deep-fry them in very hot vegetable oil for a few seconds until they puff up. Drain and set aside.

Prepare all of the ingredients. The sauces, salt and pepper can be combined in a small bowl for convenience.

Heat a pan to fry the eggs in. Add a little oil and crack in the eggs. Fry them over medium-low heat while preparing the 2-minute noodles.

Heat 1 tablespoon of oil in a wok over medium-high heat. Add the garlic, pork and bird's eye chillies and stir-fry until the pork changes colour.

Add the carrot, white cabbage and greens and stir-fry for about 30 seconds.

Add the drained noodles and combined sauces, salt and pepper. Stir-fry until well combined and heated through.

Place the noodles on serving plates and top each plate with a fried egg and krupuk. Serve with some sambal asli or another type of chilli sauce on the side.

Alternatives & Variations
- Use light soy sauce instead of kecap asin.
- For a quicker and healthier (though not quite as tasty) version of krupuk, microwave them for about 20 seconds or until puffed and crisp.
- For vegetarian Mee Goreng, omit the pork and add extra vegetables such as green (French) beans.

Nasi Goreng [Indonesian Fried Rice]

Nasi Goreng is one of the quintessential Indonesian dishes and there are countless versions of it. As well as being very tasty, Nasi Goreng is an inexpensive dish. I think it is best when served with sambal asli, a very hot chilli sauce that can be found on just about every restaurant table in Indonesia. It is available from most Asian food stores.

Ingredients

2 large or 6 small krupuk (prawn crackers), optional
1 tablespoon oyster sauce
1½ tablespoons tomato sauce
2 teaspoons salty soy sauce (kecap asin)
½ teaspoon sugar
Salt and pepper, to taste
2 eggs
2 teaspoons butter or vegetable oil
3 garlic cloves, peeled and roughly chopped
1 tablespoon onion, thinly sliced
½ cup (1½ oz/35 g) carrot, julienned
2 snake beans or 6–8 green (French) beans, thinly sliced diagonally
½ cup (2 oz/60 g) white cabbage, shredded
3 cups (11 oz/300 g) cooked rice

SERVES 2

Method

If using uncooked krupuk, deep-fry them in very hot vegetable oil for a few seconds until they puff up. Drain and set aside.

Prepare all of the ingredients in advance. The sauces, sugar, salt and pepper can be combined in a small bowl for convenience.

Heat a pan for frying the eggs. At the same time, heat a wok over medium-high heat and add the oil. Add the garlic, onion and vegetables to the wok and stir-fry for 3 minutes.

Add a little oil to the egg pan and crack in the eggs. Fry them over medium-low heat while reheating the rice.

Add the combined sauces, sugar, salt and pepper to the wok and stir until combined.

Lower the heat, add the rice and mix briefly. Now increase the heat again and stir-fry until heated through and well combined.

Pack the fried rice into a small rice bowl and turn out onto the serving plate. Top with a fried egg and krupuk. Serve with some sambal asli or other chilli sauce on the side.

Alternatives & Variations
- For meat-eaters, stir-fry some chopped chicken or pork or some peeled raw shrimp until almost cooked before adding the vegetables.
- For a quicker and healthier (though not quite as tasty) version of krupuk, microwave them for about 20 seconds or until puffed and crisp.
- Use light soy sauce instead of kecap asin.

Nasi Kuning [Balinese Yellow Rice]

In Balinese society Nasi Kuning is a ceremonial dish served at festivals and special occasions. This is a simplified but no less delicious version.

Ingredients

1 tablespoon coconut or peanut oil
3 garlic cloves, peeled and roughly chopped
1¼–1¾ in (3–4 cm) galangal, well bruised
³/₈–¾ in (1–2 cm) turmeric, well bruised
1 large or 2 small stalks lemongrass, well bruised and tied in a knot
1 salam leaf
½ teaspoon salt
½ cup (4 fl oz/125 ml) coconut milk
3 cups (11 oz/300 g) cooked rice

SERVES 2

Method

Heat a wok over medium heat and add the oil. Add the garlic and fry for 30 seconds, stirring constantly.

Add the next 5 ingredients and fry for a few minutes over medium heat until fragrant.

Add the coconut milk and cook for 1 minute. Turn off the heat.

Remove the lemongrass and salam leaf and put aside. Using a slotted spoon, remove the remaining ingredients, drain off as much liquid as possible and discard the contents of the spoon.

Add the rice, turn heat to medium, return the lemongrass and salam leaf and stir until the rice is evenly coloured and hot.

Remove the lemongrass and salam leaf before serving.

Alternatives & Variations
• Use ¾ teaspoon ground turmeric instead of fresh turmeric.
• Use dried (soaked) galangal but leave whole and remove before serving.
• Use 1 bay leaf instead of the salam leaf or omit altogether.

Bumbu Bali Ketut [Balinese Spice Paste]

This spice paste forms the flavour basis of many Balinese dishes.

Ingredients

5 large red chillies, seeded and roughly chopped

3 red bird's eye chillies, roughly chopped

¼ teaspoon black peppercorns

¼ teaspoon salt

2 garlic cloves, peeled and roughly chopped

4 shallot segments (about 2 tablespoons), roughly chopped

3 teaspoons fresh ginger, roughly chopped

3 teaspoons fresh galangal, roughly chopped

2 teaspoons fresh turmeric, roughly chopped

3 candle nuts

¼ teaspoon shrimp paste, toasted over a gas flame or wrapped in foil and lightly toasted over an electric element

2 teaspoons palm sugar, shaved or grated

MAKES ABOUT ½ CUP (4 FL OZ/125 ML)

Method

Grind the chillies, peppercorns and salt to a paste in a mortar and pestle or on a grinding stone.

Gradually add the garlic, shallots, ginger, galangal, turmeric and candle nuts (a small handful at a time) and continue to grind until fairly smooth.

Finally work in the shrimp paste and palm sugar. This spice paste can be stored in a jar in the refrigerator for up to 1 week.

Alternatives & Variations
- 1 teaspoon ground turmeric can be substituted for fresh turmeric.
- Macadamia nuts or almonds can be substituted for candle nuts.
- Omit the fresh galangal if unavailable. The spice paste will still taste good.
- Make the spice paste in a food processor.

Sambal Goreng Lombok [Fried Chilli Paste]

This sambal recipe can be served with fried chicken to make a delicious Lombok-style fried chicken or used in any dish that calls for chilli paste. The colour and quantity of the sambal will largely depend on the size and colour of the chillies and tomato used.

Ingredients

8 red bird's eye chillies
2 green bird's eye chillies
1 large garlic clove
1 small tomato, thinly sliced
¼ teaspoon shrimp paste, toasted over a
    gas flame or wrapped in foil and lightly
    toasted over an electric element
1 tablespoon coconut or peanut oil
1 very small or ¼ large lime (½ teaspoon
    juice), pips removed

MAKES ABOUT ¼ CUP (2 FL OZ/60 ML)

Method

Using a grinding stone or a mortar and pestle, grind the chillies to a paste then add the garlic and grind together until fairly smooth.

Add the tomato and shrimp paste and grind again until smooth.

Place the sambal in a small pan, turn the heat to medium and add the oil. Fry the sambal for 2 minutes, stirring constantly.

Squeeze the lime juice into the pan then add the squeezed lime shell if you wish. Stir and pour into a small bowl. Serve with grilled (broiled) or fried fish or chicken and plain rice.

Sambal Kecap [Sweet Soy and Chilli Sauce]

This sambal is excellent served with Sate Lilit Babi.

Ingredients

2 tablespoons sweet soy sauce
1 tablespoon light soy sauce
2 red bird's eye chillies, thinly sliced

MAKES ABOUT ¼ CUP (2 FL OZ/60 ML)

Method

Combine all of the ingredients. Pour the mixture into a small dish to serve.

Bumbu Kare [Indonesian Curry Paste]

This is a versatile curry paste that can be used with Kare Ayam or other Indonesian curries.

Ingredients

2 teaspoons coriander seeds
½ teaspoon cumin seeds
¼ teaspoon black peppercorns
½ teaspoon salt
1 tablespoon turmeric root, roughly
    chopped
1 tablespoon fresh ginger, roughly
    chopped
1 tablespoon fresh galangal, roughly
    chopped
3 shallot segments (about 1½
    tablespoons), roughly chopped
4 garlic cloves, peeled and roughly
    chopped
2 tablespoons coconut or peanut oil

MAKES ABOUT ¼ CUP (2 FL OZ/60 ML)

Method

Toast the coriander seeds, cumin seeds and peppercorns in a dry pan over low heat for about 4 minutes, or until fragrant.

Transfer to a mortar, add the salt and grind to a powder.

Add the turmeric, ginger and galangal and grind again. Finally add the shallots and garlic and continue to grind until you have a fairly smooth paste.

Heat a wok over medium-low heat and add the oil. Add the curry paste and fry, stirring constantly for about 5 minutes until the paste is dark in colour and the oil starts to separate.

Note: This curry paste can be stored in a jar in the refrigerator for up to 2 weeks or frozen in portions.

Alternatives & Variations
• 2 teaspoons ground turmeric can be substituted for fresh turmeric.
• Make the curry paste in a food processor.

Puding Pisang [Banana Pudding]

A delicious and simple dessert. Vanilla powder, which is used in this recipe, is available from Asian food stores at a fraction of the cost of vanilla extract or beans.

Ingredients

5 small bananas, cut in half lengthways
    and sliced into 1¾ in (4 cm) pieces
4 tablespoons sugar
½ teaspoon lemon juice
2 pandan leaves, each one roughly torn
    lengthways and tied in a knot
⅛ teaspoon vanilla powder
1 cup (8 fl oz/250 ml) water
Pinch of salt
4 tablespoons coconut milk

To Serve
Ice cream (optional)

Serves 4

Method

Put all of the ingredients except the salt and coconut milk into a saucepan.

Bring to the boil, reduce the heat and simmer for 15 minutes, until the banana is soft and swollen.

Mix together the coconut milk and salt.

Place the banana mix and syrup in serving bowls and pour 1 tablespoon of coconut milk over each serve. Serve warm or cold.

Alternatives & Variations
• Use ½ teaspoon vanilla extract or the contents of 1 vanilla bean (pod) instead of the vanilla powder.
• Pandan leaves can be omitted without making too much difference.

Pisang Goreng Kelapa [Fried Bananas with Grated Coconut]

Fried bananas are a common snack at street stalls all over Indonesia, and are a popular snack with both locals and tourists. This version has the addition of grated (shredded) coconut and palm sugar.

Ingredients

1 cup (3½ oz/100 g) plain (all-purpose)
  flour
Pinch of salt
1 egg, lightly beaten
Few drops of vanilla extract
¾ cup (6 fl oz/175 ml) cold water
Vegetable oil, for deep-frying
6 small bananas, cut in half lengthways
  and each half cut in two
¼ cup (1 oz/30 g) firmly packed grated
  coconut
½ cup (1½ oz/35 g) firmly packed grated
  palm sugar

To Serve
Vanilla ice cream

Serves 4

Method

Place the flour and salt in a bowl. Make a well in the centre, add the egg and vanilla essence and start to mix slowly, gradually adding enough water to make a thick batter.

Cover and set aside for 20 minutes.

Heat the oil in a wok over medium heat for about 12 minutes.

Stir the batter, then drop in a few pieces of banana to coat with batter. Use 2 forks to gently lift the banana pieces out, allowing excess batter to drip off them, then carefully lower them into the hot oil.

Fry the banana pieces for about 15 minutes, turning them a few times until golden brown and crisp. Do not let the oil get too hot, as slower cooking will ensure that the batter remains crisp after frying. Drain the banana pieces on paper towels.

Combine the grated coconut and brown sugar.

Place the bananas on a serving dish and dust with the coconut and sugar mixture. Serve with vanilla ice cream.

Teh Jahe [Ginger Tea]

In Indonesia, ginger tea is very popular for both its healing and refreshing qualities. Often a thermos of ginger tea is made in the morning and drunk throughout the day. Ginger tea is usually made using black tea; both black and green tea is grown in Indonesia, mainly in Java and Sumatra.

Ingredients

2¼ in (6 cm) piece fresh ginger, cut into 4 and well bruised or chopped
1¾ pints (1 litre) of prepared tea (preferably Indonesian tea)
White sugar or honey, to taste

MAKES 4–6 CUPS

Method

Place the ginger into the tea and infuse for at least 5 minutes. Stir and strain (if desired) before serving. Add sugar or honey to taste.

ACKNOWLEDGEMENTS
I would like to thank the following street stalls
and restaurants for providing recipes for the
dishes in this book: Made, Wayan and Nyoman
at Biah-Biah Warung in Ubud, Bali; Teh and her
staff of Eighty-Nine Restaurant, Krabi; F&D
King Crab Restaurant in the Geylang area; Elie
of Fernando's Coffee Shop, Tuk Tuk, Samosir
Island, Lake Toba, Sumatra; Mai of the food
centre in Malacca, Southern Malaysia; staff at
the Koh Kham resort; Pairog Boonbumroongsub
of Kra Sia Restaurant; Gao and her husband of
Lamai fresh food market, Koh Samui; Kik of
Lilly House Restaurant, Koh Samui; Friday and
Ketut of Manggala Restaurant, Padang Bai, Bali;
Lin of Marco Polo Restaurant, Samosir Island;
Nancy of Nancy's Kitchen, Malacca; Mr Cheah
of Pak Hok Famous Chicken Rice, Georgetown,
Penang; Mama Ann of Rachadamnoen food
market, Bangkok; Satri of Satri's Warung in
Ubud, Bali; Si Phen Restaurant, Intawarorot
Road, Chiang Mai; Som Song Restaurant near
Wat Sangwet, Mary Tan of Star Station 23,
Geylang Road, Singapore; 'Char Siew Master'
of Sun Yoon Kee Restaurant, Georgetown,
Penang; Mushtaq of stall number 37, Taiping
Food Centre, Taiping, Malaysia; staff at the
Tanao Road food stall, Bangkok; Noi and Mrs
Chananas of Trat; Yosman at the Ya Ya Warung,
Gili Meno, Lombok.